Poor Man's Data Dictionary

Document your database quickly, cheaply and painlessly.

Scott L. Hecht

PUBLISHED BY
CreateSpace, Inc. & Kindle Direct Publishing
Divisions of Amazon.com

ISBN-10: 149953308X
ISBN-13: 978-1499533088

Front Cover Image:
© Can Stock Photo, Inc. / dny3d

Back Cover Image:
© Can Stock Photo, Inc. / kirstypargeter

To my brother Brad, nieces Carly and Cami, and nephew Adam for always making me laugh and keeping me sane (not always an easy task).

To Jim North, for his support and help with the programming. Thank you, Jim, for years of computer-related conversations. You can stop now. ☺

To Ann R. Oliveros, Andrea Sierra, Jordan W. Klein, Jonathan Bernacki and Ryan Martinez for allowing me to take up their time with yet another one of my crazy ideas. Thank you for your help, insight, ideas, opinions and memories of a project we did so many years ago.

Contents at a Glance

Contents in Detail

Introduction

Why I Wrote This Book

Back in the day, people would tie one end of a piece of string to a child's loose tooth, the other end to a door knob, and then slam the door shut. Most programmers believe that documenting a database is just as painful, but it doesn't have to be.

The reason I created my own data dictionary process at work is simple: there were just too many databases, too many tables and too many columns to keep everything straight in my brain. Do I use *this* table or *that* view and what's the difference between them? What's the definition of *that* column and why am I not using *this* other column instead? It had become a nightmare and something needed to be done... quickly!

This book outlines the process the author and his colleagues successfully went through to create a data dictionary for every database within our small company. While the author cannot guarantee that the steps outlined herein will be a rousing success in your company, at least it can serve as a starting point for the creation of your own data dictionary process.

Who Should Read This Book

In order to keep this book as generic as possible, I do not assume what your company does, what database it uses, how many SQL programmers there are, how many database administrators there are, and so on. For example, you may be the only database administrator within your company and are solely responsible for creating and maintaining its data dictionary. But, some companies have multiple database administrators who just don't have the time to create and maintain a data dictionary, so this task must fall on another employee.

I do assume, though, that you have some knowledge of Visual Basic for Applications (VBA), PHP and/or ASP.NET, or you work with people who do have this knowledge.

With that said, this book is intended for anyone who uses a database, from the humble Microsoft Access SQL programmer to the lofty Oracle or SQL Server database administrator as well as the manager who tries to keep them both from killing each other.

If you work on multiple databases containing multiple tables and you just can't keep everything straight in your brain (welcome to the club!), then this book is for you.

If your databases change so often that new tables or fields are added or old ones are modified frequently, then this book is for you.

If you've ever attempted to train a new employee on how to use the database and your training materials consist of documents photocopied so many times that hundreds of black dots cover the important bits, then this book is for you.

If your salespeople are having trouble understanding just what's contained within the company's databases, then this book is for you. When your salespeople fully comprehend what's contained within the databases, they can potentially sell more reports, data marts, and so on. More is good!

Finally, if you need to create a data dictionary that will be delivered to a client along with, say, a data mart, then this book is also for you.

Organization of This Book

To keep this book *painless*, as stated in the subtitle, this book is brief. There are only eight total chapters containing the following information:

Chapter 1, *The Data Dictionary Explained* introduces the concept of a data dictionary, why you should create one as well as the benefits of doing so. This chapter concludes with an overview of the entire data dictionary creation process.

Chapter 2, *The Data Dictionary and Microsoft Word* explains why I recommend using Microsoft Word (for all you haters out there!) in the creation of your data dictionary as opposed to some other software. This chapter also introduces the metadata tables available in Oracle, SQL Server, Teradata, and MySQL as well as how to pull the appropriate information from them in order to populate my freely available Microsoft Word Data Dictionary Template.

Chapter 3, *Dictionary Content Meetings* explains what a dictionary content meeting is, who should attend, how often they should occur, what occurs during them, who should lead them, and so on.

Chapter 4, *Loading the Data Dictionary into the Database* explains how to use one of several Visual Basic for Applications (VBA) subroutines provided with the Microsoft Word Data Dictionary Template to unload the information contained within the document itself into tables in the database. This chapter also discusses what those tables look like and how to view them once they've been loaded into the target database.

Chapter 5, *Displaying the Data Dictionary* outlines a variety of ways you can display the data dictionary via web pages using Microsoft Active Server Pages (ASP.NET) or PHP, Microsoft SharePoint and MediaWiki (the software behind Wikipedia) as well as a brief discussion of who should be able to access the information contained within the data dictionary.

Chapter 6, *Maintaining the Data Dictionary* explains several ways you can painlessly maintain your data dictionary in order to keep it up-to-date (or, at least, as up-to-date as possible).

Chapter 7, *Extending the Data Dictionary* explains why you may want to extend the data dictionary to include additional information such as business rules, functions, stored procedures and so on.

Chapter 8, *Data Dictionary Software* goes over a variety of free and not-so-free data dictionary software available out there in the world which can be use along with or instead of the method described in this book

The Goal of this Book

By the end of the book, you should be able to pull all of the tables and fields within a single database into the Microsoft Word Data Dictionary Template; schedule dictionary content meetings whose sole purpose is to describe all of the tables and their columns; unload the completed Microsoft Word Data Dictionary Template into several data dictionary tables in a database of your choice; display the data dictionary tables using the software of your choice; and, finally, create a process used to maintain the data dictionary so that it stays reasonably up-to-date.

Support

You can find the freely downloadable copy of my Microsoft Word Data Dictionary Template on my personal website at www.sheepsqueezers.com (…I know, I know, it's a silly name…). This template contains several VBA subroutines to pull schema information from an Oracle or SQL Server database, as well as unload the completed template into tables in either one of those databases or one of your own choosing.

While the subroutines provided are geared towards Oracle and SQL Server, you can easily modify the VBA code to pull from – as well as push to – other databases as long as that database has rich metadata information available. For example, you can use Oracle's ALL_TAB_COLUMNS dictionary view in order to pull all of the columns and their corresponding data types for one or more tables.   In SQL Server, the INFORMATION_SCHEMA.COLUMNS dictionary view serves a similar purpose.   If your database does not give you access to this type of information, the Microsoft Word Data Dictionary Template won't fill in the document correctly.

Finally, if your own data dictionary project is a success, please feel free to e-mail me at *comments@ sheepsqueezers.com*. While I cannot answer specific questions, I would **LOVE** to hear about your own data dictionary triumphs.

Caution and Warning

In order to prevent unexpected events (i.e., surprises), please make sure to read the entire book through once and perform a small test of the entire process on your own with a handful of tables.   By doing this, you'll confirm that the entire process works as expected.

Chapter 1 - *The Data Dictionary Explained*

What is a Data Dictionary?

A *data dictionary*, as far as we're concerned, is a place to store information used to enumerate and describe the tables as well as the fields within one or more databases.   This information is also known as *metadata*, or *data about data*. Occasionally, a data dictionary is also referred to as a *data repository* or, if you really want to be high-brow, a *metadata repository*.

Having access to this metadata allows a SQL programmer to easily determine if a particular table or field is the correct one to use within his or her SQL query.

A data dictionary can be stored in one of several places. In this book, we describe how to use Microsoft Word to, at least initially, quickly create table and column descriptions as well as how to transfer this metadata to data dictionary tables within a database.

But, you are not limited to those storage types.   For example, SQL Server has an extended properties facility useful for storing table and column descriptions within the database itself. Unfortunately, these descriptions need to be placed into the extended properties and not every database administrator has the time to create and maintain these descriptions.   You can achieve similar results in Oracle by using its COMMENT statement to associate a string with a table, column, etc. We discuss both SQL Server's extended properties and Oracle's COMMENT statement later in the book.

Finally, there are several pieces of software available to help you create and maintain your data dictionary. For example, Redgate SQL Doc and Adivo TechWriter both use SQL Server's extended properties, but both cost between US$179 and US$369 per seat (as of the writing of this book). We talk more about these two pieces of software as well as several more in Chapter 8, *Data Dictionary Software*. Please remember, though, that one goal of this book is to help you complete your data dictionary project *cheaply* which is why Microsoft Word is recommended, at least initially, and not these other products.

Why Create a Data Dictionary?

Twenty years ago or so I worked for a company that employed Pete. Don't get me wrong, Pete was a nice enough guy, had been at the company for decades and was a fount of information. But, if you asked Pete a question, his answer would provide you with *just enough* information to answer your *exact* question, no more, no less. This forced you to continually go back to him for the next sliver of information. Needless to say, in today's fast paced world of the internet and microwavable soups, this cannot be.

Nowadays, programmers have instantaneous access to all sorts of online documentation via the internet. Why shouldn't this same instantaneous access be true of the metadata within your company's databases? By creating a data dictionary, you give your employees instantaneous access to up-to-date information contained within the data dictionary. For the most part, gone will be the days your senior SQL programmers and database administrators will waste answering tedious questions on what a particular field means or which table is the correct one to use.

Benefits of Creating a Data Dictionary

As stated above, one benefit of creating a data dictionary is to speed up the process of acclimatizing a new SQL programmer or database administrator to the tables and fields within the databases in your company minimizing handholding by the employee tasked with performing the training.

If your company has salespeople who work with clients, in order to sell more reports, data marts, etc., the salesperson should have a reasonable idea as to what each database contains. The data dictionary can quickly bring a new, or even seasoned, salesperson up-to-speed as to the information available to sell.

Who are the Stakeholders?

When my colleagues and I created our company's data dictionary, we decided to do the project outside of normal project management channels. This means that we had no project number, no project manager, no timelines, no goals, no dependencies, etc. As you can well imagine, IT WAS GLORIOUS...until we made the data dictionary publicly available to the entire company. Our manager was furious because we gave *everybody in the entire company* access to the data dictionary rather than the groups he deemed deserving such as the database administrators, SQL programmers, etc.   He felt that giving access to the salespeople was unnecessary and potentially problematic, a point I still strongly disagree with. (We discuss this issue in Chapter 5, *Displaying the Data Dictionary*.)

Now, in order to avoid this with your own data dictionary project, you can either make it a *real* project or find one or more stakeholders who agree with the project's goals and who are willing to back you.

Personally, I don't recommend making the data dictionary project a *real* project and I explain why later on in the book.

As far as stakeholders go, your immediate boss could be the stakeholder. The manager of the database administrators could be a stakeholder since his direct reports will benefit greatly from the data dictionary. In any case, you should find at least one senior manager willing to *get your back* (as the young kids say) especially if the project is not *on the books*.

Overview of the Data Dictionary Process

In this section, I describe the entire data dictionary process. In subsequent chapters, I go into much more detail.

1. *Prepare the Microsoft Word Data Dictionary Template*
    a. Download the Microsoft Word Data Dictionary Template from www.sheepsqueezers.com and open it up in Microsoft Word.
    b. Click on the Developer menu and click on the Visual Basic menu item on the ribbon to bring up the Visual Basic Editor.
    c. There are two pieces of SQL code used to pull metadata from the dictionary tables, one for Oracle and the other for SQL Server. Grab the appropriate piece of SQL code, modify it, and run it in the appropriate software to check that it works properly. For Oracle, you can use Oracle SQL Developer, SQL*Plus, Toad or other tool of your choice. For SQL Server, you'll probably just stick with SQL Server Management Studio.
    d. Modify the database connection string to pull data from the appropriate database and account (or schema). For Oracle, this can be run using your own login credentials. For SQL Server, you can use either Windows Authentication or force in a SQL Server username and password.
    e. Delete the contents of the entire Microsoft Word document to ensure a clean document *before* initially populating the document with the data dictionary contents.
    f. Run the appropriate Visual Basic for Applications (VBA) subroutine based on whether you're pulling data from Oracle or SQL Server. If you're pulling from another database, please copy and paste one of these subroutines and modify it to work with your database.
    g. Once the subroutine has completed, the Microsoft Word document will be filled in with all of the tables within the selected database as well

as all of the columns, data types and nullability formatted nicely.

2. *Prepare for the data dictionary content meetings*

   a. Determine who should attend the data dictionary content meetings. These meetings should consist of at most five or six people of differing levels of seniority and knowledge of the tables and fields. Don't forget to invite at least one recently hired SQL programmer so that if one of your descriptions is not clear you'll know immediately.

   b. Schedule several content meetings so that they work around everybody's current workload and deliverable schedule.

   c. Ensure that you've scheduled the dictionary content meetings in a room that has an overhead projector (or analog) This will ensure that everyone sees the Microsoft Word Data Dictionary Template as it is being filled in.

   d. You should invite the stakeholder to, at least, the first meeting and then make him/her optional for the remaining meetings.

   e. Over the next few days or weeks, continue to fill in the Microsoft Word document with descriptions of the tables and fields during the subsequent dictionary content meetings.

3. *Unload the completed Microsoft Word Data Dictionary Template to the database*

   a. Save a copy of the filled in Microsoft Word Data Dictionary Template as a backup.

   b. Next, go back into the Visual Basic for Applications Editor and locate the appropriate subroutine that unloads the document.

   c. Since each Microsoft Word Data Dictionary Template represents the tables and columns from a *specific* database, ensure that you update the variable intDBID to represent the database. It is set to one by default which is fine for your first database, but will need to be incremented for all subsequent databases.

    d. Copy the SQL CREATE TABLE statements for the data dictionary tables. These statements should be modified for and executed on your target database so that the tables are ready to be loaded. These statements are provided for both Oracle and SQL Server and will have to be modified if you're using a different database.

    e. Modify the connection string to communicate with the target database.

    f. Execute the unload subroutine. Once completed, the tables should contain the same information as in the document itself.

    g. Please check the data dictionary tables themselves to ensure that all tables and fields are filled in properly.

4. *Determine the Desired Display for the Data Dictionary*

    a. Once the template has been filled in, you can save the document in one of several formats: Microsoft Word document (.docx, without the VBA!), Adobe Acrobat Reader (.pdf), Rich Text Format (.rtf), and so on. These can be placed on your company's intranet, distributed via e-mail or, heaven forbid, printed out.

    b. You can display the data dictionary as webpages using one of several solutions such as ASP.NET via IIS, PHP via Apache, and so on. This type of solution would make use the data dictionary tables rather than the Microsoft Word Data Dictionary Template itself, of course.

    c. You can display the data dictionary as wiki pages using the same software used by Wikipedia, MediaWiki. This requires that wiki pages be created for each table based on the completed Microsoft Word Data Dictionary Template.

    d. You can display the data dictionary using the wiki feature in Microsoft SharePoint. This requires that wiki pages be created for each table based on the completed Microsoft Word Data Dictionary Template.

e. If using Microsoft SQL Server, you can use the stored procedures associated with the extended properties feature in order to populate the extended properties in the database itself. This will allow you to use software such as Redgate SQL Doc, Adivo TechWriter, and so on.

f. If using Oracle, you can use the COMMENT statement to make comments on tables or columns.

g. ...and so on...

5. *Maintain the Data Dictionary*

a. Every so often, tables are added, dropped or modified as well as databases created or destroyed. Your data dictionary needs to be up-to-date for it to be useful, so you'll need to determine who will maintain the data dictionary. This may not necessarily be a member of the SQL programmers or database administrators department, but another department such as the Production or Reference Data Management (RDM) departments.

b. Changes to the database should be communicated to the maintainer of the data dictionary who can either update the Microsoft Word Data Dictionary Template, the Wiki site, the SQL Server extended properties, Oracle COMMENTs, etc.

c. Rather than Dictionary Content Meetings, changes can be requested via e-mail to the maintainer of the data dictionary.

Chapter 2 - *The Data Dictionary and Microsoft Word*

Why Use Microsoft Word?

I can hear you all screaming, "MICROSOFT WORD? ARE YOU CRAZY? I'D SOONER EAT HAGGIS THAN USE MICROSOFT WORD!"

Others may be asking, "So, Mr. Fancy Pants, why not use Microsoft Excel or Microsoft Access instead?"

Still others may be questioning, "Wouldn't a web interface be a better way to go instead? This is the 21st century, ya know!"

And still other others, "Surely there must be software out there that we can use instead of *putrid* Microsoft Word?" (There are…and please don't call me Shirley.)

Lemme 'splain.

I chose Microsoft Word for several reasons:

1. Using Visual Basic for Applications (VBA), Microsoft Word can automatically create a nicely formatted document containing the tables and columns from the database's own dictionary catalogue (Oracle's ALL_TAB_COLUMNS and Microsoft SQL Server's INFORMATION_SCHEMA.COLUMNS, say).

2. During the dictionary content meetings, this nicely formatted document will be displayed using an overhead projector (or analog) so that the team members can see the descriptions being entered. The formatted document is clean and easy to read which is beneficial during these meetings.

3. Using Visual Basic for Applications (VBA), Microsoft Word can unload the information contained within the

    document itself directly into database tables.   Once these tables are loaded, it's your choice what to do with them next.

4. A Microsoft Word document can be saved in any one of a number of formats such as Adobe Acrobat Reader (.pdf), Rich Text Format (.rtf), and so on. This document can be sent to internal as well as external clients and is sufficient as a physical data dictionary since it is already nicely formatted.

5. Finally, Microsoft Word is, most likely, already installed on your computer and is effectively **free**. No additional outlay of money is needed. Huzzah!

While Microsoft Excel and Access could be used, these tools are difficult to read when projected using an overhead projector. Also, filling in cells on an Excel spreadsheet or in Access can be an editor's nightmare. Microsoft Word allows you to easily enter textual descriptions using a familiar interface. Not to mention that creating a nicely formatted document to be sent to a client is much easier when using Microsoft Word. Would you send a client an Adobe Acrobat Reader file produced from Excel or Access? Using Excel or Access flies in the face of the word *painlessly* in the subtitle of my book.

While a web site sounds ideal, who's going to build it? And how long will it take for them to get to it with all of the work on the web department's plate? Not to mention all of those changes to the website you'll want once you see it live. This flips the bird at the word *quickly* in the subtitle of my book.

And while there's a plethora of software products available to help you create and maintain your own data dictionary (see Chapter 8, *Data Dictionary Software*), who's going to learn the software? You? Do you have time for that? And when you move the data dictionary maintenance process to another department, who's going to learn the software then? And, don't forget that some data dictionary software costs actual-real-live moolah and is sold per user. This can really add up and spits on the word *cheaply* in the subtitle of my book.

Regardless of whether you agree or disagree with my reasons for using Microsoft Word, it does serve its purpose as middleware in the data dictionary creation process.[i] With that said, you may want to peruse Chapter 8, *Data Dictionary Software* to see if one of those applications would be better suited to your needs rather than the method outlined in this book.

Database Metadata Availability

All major databases have tables or views giving you access to metadata on the tables and columns contained within each individual database.

The metadata contained within these tables or views varies, but usually consists of table name, column name, data type, whether the column is null or not (nullability), and so on. Some databases may have more metadata available, some less and some none.

In Oracle, you can use the dictionary views such as ALL_TAB_COLUMNS for a list of tables, columns, data types, and more.

In SQL Server, you can use the INFORMATION_SCHEMA views in order to access the database metadata.   For example, INFORMATION_SCHEMA.COLUMNS is similar to Oracle's ALL_TAB_COLUMNS.

MySQL uses the INFORMATION_SCHEMA.COLUMNS view as well, but Teradata uses the DBC.COLUMNS view.

Please check the documentation for your database to determine which tables or views to use to pull metadata information.

Now, I used this metadata information to create a SQL query that's used by the VBA subroutines tasked with initially populating the Microsoft Word Data Dictionary Template. For these subroutines, the query is limited to table names, column names, data types, and nullability, but you can include any additional information you want if you feel that the dictionary should contain it. If you decide to change the template you'll have to modify the VBA code behind it!

For example, below is the SQL query submitted to SQL Server in order to pull the metadata information used to populate the Microsoft Word Data Dictionary Template. Note that the emboldened code below subsets the query to my desired tables, but you can modify this as you see fit.

```
SELECT A.TABLE_NAME,
       A.COLUMN_NAME,
       CASE
        WHEN A.DATA_TYPE='int' THEN 'INT'
        WHEN A.DATA_TYPE='bigint' THEN 'BIGINT'
        WHEN A.DATA_TYPE='smallint' THEN 'SMALLINT'
        WHEN A.DATA_TYPE='tinyint' THEN 'TINYINT'
        WHEN A.DATA_TYPE='float' THEN 'FLOAT'
        WHEN A.DATA_TYPE='real' THEN 'REAL'
        WHEN A.DATA_TYPE='date' THEN 'DATE'
        WHEN A.DATA_TYPE='smalldatetime'
                                   THEN 'SMALLDATETIME'
        WHEN A.DATA_TYPE='datetime' THEN 'DATETIME'
        WHEN A.DATA_TYPE='datetime2' THEN 'DATETIME2'
        WHEN A.DATA_TYPE='time' THEN 'TIME'
        WHEN A.DATA_TYPE='varchar' THEN 'VARCHAR('
       + CONVERT(VARCHAR,CHARACTER_MAXIMUM_LENGTH) + ')'
       END AS DATTYP,
       CASE WHEN A.IS_NULLABLE='YES' THEN 'NULL'
            WHEN A.IS_NULLABLE='NO' THEN 'NOT NULL'
       END AS NULLRES,
       DENSE_RANK() OVER (ORDER BY A.TABLE_NAME)
                                        AS TABLE_NUM,
       COUNT(*) OVER (PARTITION BY A.TABLE_NAME)
                                        AS TOTAL_COLS,
       B.TOTAL_TABLES
       FROM TESTDB.INFORMATION_SCHEMA.COLUMNS A,
           (SELECT COUNT(DISTINCT TABLE_NAME)
                                        AS TOTAL_TABLES
             FROM TESTDB.INFORMATION_SCHEMA.COLUMNS
             WHERE TABLE_NAME IN
                   ('CANDYBAR_FACT','RESPONDENT_DIM',
```

```
                        'CANDYBAR_DIM','CANDYMFR_DIM',
                        'DATE_DIM')) B
        WHERE A.TABLE_NAME IN
                    ('CANDYBAR_FACT','RESPONDENT_DIM',
                     'CANDYBAR_DIM','CANDYMFR_DIM',
                     'DATE_DIM')
        ORDER BY A.TABLE_NAME,A.ORDINAL_POSITION;
```

When using SQL Server Management Studio, the results of this query is as follows (abbreviated output):

TABLE NAME	COLUMN NAME	DATTYP	NULLRES
RESPONDENT_DIM	RESPONDENT_ID	INT	NOTNULL
RESPONDENT_DIM	RESPONDENT_NAME	VARCHAR(50)	NULL
RESPONDENT_DIM	RESPONDENT_ADDR	VARCHAR(100)	NULL
RESPONDENT_DIM	RESPONDENT_CITY	VARCHAR(50)	NULL
RESPONDENT_DIM	RESPONDENT_STATE	VARCHAR(2)	NULL
RESPONDENT_DIM	RESPONDENT_ZIPCODE	VARCHAR(9)	NULL
RESPONDENT_DIM	RESPONDENT_PHONE_NUM	VARCHAR(10)	NULL
RESPONDENT_DIM	RESPONDENT_GENDER	VARCHAR(1)	NULL
RESPONDENT_DIM	RESPONDENT_DOB	DATE	NULL

Let's go through this SQL query line by line:

First, I request both the TABLE_NAME field as well as the COLUMN_NAME field, both of which will be used to indicate the name of the table as well as name the corresponding fields within each table. 'Nuf said.

Next, to create the column DATTYP, a CASE Statement is used to turn the DATA_TYPE column into a nicer format. With Oracle, the data types are all capitalized, but in SQL Server they are in lower case. In order to be consistent across databases, I decided to use a CASE Statement to ensure everything is formatted nicely. For example, I create the text for VARCHAR providing the maximum character length in parentheses (for example, VARCHAR(30)).

Next, the column NULLRES is created based on the IS_NULLABLE column. Instead of printing the words YES or NO in the template, I prefer NULL or NOT NULL to indicate column nullability.

Next, in order to give each individual table a unique number, the column TABLE_NUM is created using the DENSE_ RANK() analytic function ordered by the name of the table. So, despite the number of columns in each table, the first table will be assigned a 1, the next table a 2, and so on, based on ascending alphabetical ordering of the table name.

Next, the column TABLE_COLS is created using the analytic function COUNT(*) OVER (PARTITION BY A.TABLE_ NAME) statement which counts the number of columns *within* each table.   So, for the RESPONDENT_DIM table shown above, this column would contain the number 9 for each corresponding row indicating that this particular table contains nine columns in total.

The column TOTAL_TABLES is created so that it contains the total number of distinct tables. This column is always 5 in the SQL query above since it subsets for exactly five tables. Note that, unlike Oracle, SQL Server 2012 and prior do not allow you to use the DISTINCT keyword when using analytic functions. For Oracle, I use the code COUNT(DISTINCT A.TABLE_NAME) OVER () AS TOTAL_TABLES instead and drop the query aliased to B.   For your database, you may have to be just as creative.

Finally, the INFORMATION_SCHEMA.COLUMNS view is queried subsetting based on the desired tables. The resulting data is sorted by TABLE_NAME and ORDINAL_ POSITION. The ORDINAL_POSITION column contains a value indicating the location the column appears within the original CREATE TABLE statement which created the table.

As stated above, you can add additional columns to this SQL query based on any additional information you'd like added to the Microsoft Word Data Dictionary Template.   Note that you'll have to modify the VBA code in order to place additional information on the page, but it's not that difficult.

Populating the Data Dictionary Template

Below are the detailed steps you must follow in order to populate the Microsoft Word Data Dictionary Template with tables and columns from your database.

Note that there are four subroutines within the template:

1. PullOracleTables – this subroutine pulls the metadata information from Oracle's data dictionary and populates the Microsoft Word Data Dictionary Template. This is run to *initially* populate the template.
2. PullSQLServerTables – this subroutine pulls the metadata information from SQL Server's data dictionary and populates the Microsoft Word Data Dictionary. This is run to *initially* populate the template.
3. UnloadDocumentAndLoadToOracleDB – this subroutine *unloads* the information contained within the Microsoft Word Data Dictionary Template and *loads* it into tables in Oracle. This is run *after* the dictionary content meetings have completed.
4. UnloadDocumentAndLoadToSQLServerDB – this subroutine *unloads* the information contained within the Microsoft Word Data Dictionary Template and *loads* it into tables in SQL Server. This is run *after* the dictionary content meetings have completed.

We talk more about the Unload* routines in a later chapter.

Both PullOracleTables and PullSQLServerTables make use of the class clsMetadataColumnInfo in order to hold each row's metadata information. This class contains the following attributes:

```
Public strTABLE_NAME As String
Public strCOLUMN_NAME As String
Public strDATTYP As String
Public strNULLRES As String
Public intTABLE_NUM As Integer
Public intTOTAL_COLS As Integer
```

Note that you will have to add additional attributes to this class if you add additional metadata information.

Here are the steps to perform:

1. Download the Microsoft Word Data Dictionary Template from www.sheepsqueezers.com and open it in Microsoft Word.

2. Click on the Developer menu and click on the Visual Basic menu item on the ribbon to bring up the Visual Basic Editor.

3. There are two pieces of SQL code used to pull metadata from the dictionary tables, one for Oracle and the other for SQL Server. These are commented out (in Visual Basic, comments begin with an apostrophe). Grab the appropriate piece of SQL code, modify it, and run it in the appropriate software to check that it works properly. For Oracle, you can use Oracle's SQL Developer, SQL*Plus, Toad or other tool of your choice. For SQL Server, you should use Microsoft SQL Server Management Studio. Once you get this code to work correctly, modify the Visual Basic string strSQL to reflect the change(s) you made, if any.

4. Modify the database connection string to pull data from the appropriate database and account (or schema). For Oracle, this can be run using your own login credentials.   For SQL Server, you can use either Windows authentication or force in a SQL Server username and password. I have created a Visual Basic for Applications form, called frmPull, which contains two command buttons: btnPullOracle (shown at the top of the image below) and btnPullSQLServer (shown at the bottom of the image below).

If you **double-click** on the appropriate button, you will be taken directly to the associated code in the VBA editor that will be executed *if that button were pushed when the form is run.* For instance, double-clicking on btnPullOracle will take you to the click event btnPullOracle_Click. Within this code, you can enter in your Oracle username, password, data source, server, etc. Similar comments apply to the SQL Server button.

5. Delete the contents of the entire Microsoft Word document to ensure a clean document before creating the initial data dictionary contents. Then, select all and select an appropriate font and font size. For me, I like Verdana 9 point.

6. Run the form frmPull by clicking the F5 button in the Visual Basic Editor. Then, click on the appropriate button based on whether you are pulling data from Oracle or SQL Server. If you're pulling from another database, copy and paste one of these subroutines and modify it, as well as the form, in order for it to work with your database.

7. Once the subroutine has completed, the Microsoft Word document will be filled in with all of the tables within the selected database as well as all of the columns, their data types and their nullability formatted nicely. For example, here is what one of my tables, CANDYBAR_DIM, looks like when the template is *initially* populated:

Table: CANDYBAR_DIM		
COLUMN NAME	**DATABASE DATA TYPE**	**NULLABILITY**
CANDYBAR_ID	INT	NOT NULL
CANDYBAR_NAME	VARCHAR(50)	NULL
CANDYBAR_MFR_ID	INT	NULL
CANDYBAR_WEIGHT_OZ	FLOAT	NULL

Table Description

Enter description of this table here.

Column Description

- CANDYBAR_ID: Enter description of this column here.
- CANDYBAR_NAME: Enter description of this column here.
- CANDYBAR_MFR_ID: Enter description of this column here.
- CANDYBAR_WEIGHT_OZ: Enter description of this column here.

Caveats

- Caveat #1: Enter description of caveat here.

Note that the text *Enter description of this table here*, *Enter description of this column here* and *Caveat #1: Enter description of caveat here*, shown above, can all be changed to the text you desire within the subroutines. Remember that you will be filling in this information during the dictionary content meetings, so make your life easy and replace these strings with appropriate text. For example, for the columns, I usually set the text to *This field contains* and then fill in the rest during the dictionary content meeting. This prevents me from having to constantly type *This field contains*. For the table description, I usually set the text to *This table contains*. Since only one caveat will be generated automatically when the Microsoft Word Data Dictionary Template is first populated, I usually set the text to *None* and then change it, if necessary.

Note that you may want to include additional information such as indexes, primary keys, functions, stored procedures, and so on. We discuss extending the Microsoft Word Data Dictionary Template in a later chapter.

8. Finally, save the populated Microsoft Data Dictionary Template with an appropriate name such as the name of the database.

You are now ready to hold data dictionary contents meetings to fill in the populated template. We describe dictionary contents meetings in the next chapter.

Caution and Warning

First, make sure to first clear out the entire Word document so that no previous text appears before pulling from the database. Next, highlight the entire document and select Verdana 9-point font. Although the VBA code contains code to select for a font and font-size, that code does not seem to function properly.

Second, when filling in the table, column and caveat descriptions, make sure you limit the text size to 2000 characters or less. This is because, as discussed in Chapter 4, *Loading the Dictionary into the Database*, I limit the number of characters being loaded into the data dictionary tables. Naturally, you can increase this size if your descriptions are particularly Proustian.

Third, the description of each table in the Table Description section should be contained within a single paragraph, not multiple paragraphs. If your ultimate goal is to display the dictionary within a web browser, you may want to enter an HTML <br> tag to force a line break, but please have a conversation with a web programmer first before filling in the populated template with this tag.

Chapter 3 - *Dictionary Content Meetings*

What's a Dictionary Content Meeting?

Once you've initially populated the Microsoft Word Data Dictionary Template (see previous chapter), you're ready to hold dictionary content meetings to fill it in.

A Dictionary Content Meeting is a limited number of recurring meetings used to fill in the populated Microsoft Word Data Dictionary Template with table, column, and caveat descriptions.

Who Should Attend?

In order for the Dictionary Content Meetings to be effective, you need to select attendees with a variety of experience and, possibly, from different departments.

First, you need to ensure that the stakeholder is invited to, at least, the first meeting. The stakeholder can be optional for the remaining meetings.

Next, invite at least one database administrator, if possible, since he/she is intimately familiar with the tables and columns and may know important caveats that should be placed in the data dictionary.

You should also invite several SQL programmers with varying lengths of experience. The SQL programmer or manager in charge of training new hires should be asked to attend as well.

You may also want to invite one or more data analysts or statisticians in your company since they may have more detailed knowledge of the tables and columns in the database.

You may want to include at least one person from your Reference Data Management (RDM) department, if your company has such a department. If not, invite someone who plays a similar role in the company if you feel that he or she would lend insight into the columns. For example, in the pharmaceutical industry, the RDM department has an intimate understanding of ICD-9 diagnosis and procedure codes. Since these codes appear in one or more columns within one or more tables in the database, inviting a member of the RDM department will lend a more detailed understanding of these columns.

Finally, make sure that you involve at least one new hire in the meetings. If any definition is not clear, the new hire should tell you, although a diffident new hire may need to be prompted.

How Often Should They Occur?

Dictionary Content Meetings can occur as often as you like and depend on the availability of the people attending the meetings. When my colleagues and I scheduled our Dictionary Content Meetings, we met twice a week, once during lunch and once for two hours after work. This allowed us to completely fill in the template in a few weeks. Naturally, if you can meet more often, then by all means do so.

Meeting twice a week may not be possible for you and your colleagues due to a heavy workload, people out sick, on vacation, and so on. During the first meeting, you should all decide the frequency, day(s) and time(s) you want to meet. This should be scheduled through Microsoft Outlook, or similar software, as a recurring meeting so no one forgets to attend.

Note that these Dictionary Content Meetings should not be dragged out until everybody in the meeting dies of old age. The whole purpose of these meetings is to *quickly* fill in the template in order to make the data dictionary available as soon as possible. With that said, you do want the best possible descriptions of the tables and columns as you can get, so a single meeting probably won't cut the mustard.

On the flip side, scheduling Dictionary Content Meetings as ongoing and never-ending is probably not a good idea either. After the first meeting, see how many tables you all fill in and, based on that, estimate the number of meetings you'll need.

Where Should We Meet?

The Dictionary Contents Meetings should be held in a conference room with an overhead projector (or analog) that can be attached to your laptop. This will allow you to project the populated Microsoft Word Data Dictionary Template onto a wall or screen for the Dictionary Content Meeting attendees to see as you're typing in table and column definitions. This will allow the other attendees to not only hear the definition, but see it as well allowing for any spelling mistakes to be caught then and there.

Who Should Lead the Meeting?

Since you're the one who took enough interest in the subject to purchase this book and read it up to this point, I nominate you! Woo-hoo! With that said, you should be able to lead meetings, like typing a lot (or, at least, tolerate it), and have some familiarity with SQL and VBA to do the tasks outlined in the book (or find someone who can help you).

Your idea, your project! Okay, my idea, but it's still your project!

What Occurs During the Meeting?

During each Dictionary Content Meeting, you'll use the conference room projector to display the populated Microsoft Word Data Dictionary Template onto a wall or screen. With the help of the attendees, fill in the definitions for each table and column as well as any caveats you feel are necessary.

For example, the definition of the table CANDYBAR_DIM could be "This dimension table contains a unique list of candy bars identified by the field CANDYBAR_ID." There may be some tables that are deprecated and rather than just remove them from the populated template, fill in the description something like this "DEPRECATED TABLE! DO NOT USE! This table contains..." Note that you should still fill in the table and column descriptions just in case someone has to modify an old piece of SQL code that depends on the deprecated table.

Note that the SQL code used to populate the template (see previous chapter) may also return views as well as tables. If the object you're defining in the populated template is a *view* rather than a *table*, modify the description to reflect that: "This view contains...".

The column CANDYBAR_ID could be defined as "CANDYBAR_ID: This primary key field contains a unique number assigned to each candy bar specified in the CANDYBAR_NAME field and takes on values such as 1, 2, 3, and so on." Take note that I indicate that this field is a primary key column as well as display a few of the values that the column takes on: 1, 2, 3, etc. As another example, the column CANDYBAR_NAME could be defined as "CANDYBAR_NAME: This field contains the full name of the candy bar and takes on values such as Mounds, Hershey Bar, Krackel, and so on." By taking the time to fill in a few values within the column, the person reading the definition will gain a greater understanding of the column itself and whether it's the correct column to use.

One caveat for this table may be "Caveat #1: The prices indicated in the column CANDYBAR_PRICE_USD are from 2012 and do not reflect current candy bar prices." Although this caveat could be added to the column's definition instead, placing it in the caveats section may give it more importance.

Please ensure that you leave the column names followed by a colon as well as the numbered caveats followed by a colon. We talk more about this in a later chapter.

Note that there's no need to proceed from the top of the populated template to the bottom. Feel free to skip around the template as you see fit. It may be better to fill in the tables with the fewest columns first and then tackle the larger tables in subsequent dictionary content meetings.

One thing you should *not* do is attempt to fill in the populated template by yourself since you'll almost invariably obtain better definitions and insights when your colleagues are involved in the process.

Finally, in my experience, some definitions will prompt a discussion (argument?) between several attendees which usually leads to a better description of the tables, columns and caveats. But, please ensure that the discussion of a single column doesn't spiral out of control and take over the entire meeting. Remember: the goal is to fill in the populated template in a reasonable amount of time, or *quickly*.

Chapter 4 - *Loading the Dictionary into the Database*

Why Load the Dictionary into the Database?

In the previous chapters, we discussed how to pull metadata from the database to populate the Microsoft Word Data Dictionary Template as well as how to hold Dictionary Content Meetings to fill it in.

Now that these tasks are complete, it's time to unload the table and column definitions from the completed template and store them in the database.

So, why are we doing this? In order to display the data dictionary using, say, ASP.NET or PHP, you need to have this data loaded into a database. This will make your web programmer's life a little easier. In the next chapter, we discuss a variety of ways to display the contents of the data dictionary tables.

Create the Data Dictionary Tables

Before attempting to load the contents of the completed template into the database, you'll need to create the tables used to hold this information. You'll find the SQL code for both Oracle and SQL Server within the Visual Basic code in the Microsoft Word Data Dictionary Template. If you're using a different database, modify the SQL CREATE TABLE statements appropriately. I've reproduced the SQL Server version of the SQL code below:

```
CREATE TABLE DATADICT_DB_DEFN(DB_ID int,
                              DB_NAME varchar(30))

CREATE TABLE DATADICT_TABLE_NAME(DB_ID int,
                                 TABLE_ID int,
                                 TABLE_NAME varchar(30))

CREATE TABLE DATADICT_TABLE_DESC(DB_ID int,
                                 TABLE_ID int,
```

```
                                    TABLE_DESC varchar(2000))

CREATE TABLE DATADICT_COLUMN_DEFN(DB_ID int,
                                  TABLE_ID int,
                                  COLUMN_ID int,
                                  COLUMN_NAME varchar(30),
                                  DATA_TYPE varchar(20),
                                  NULLABILITY varchar(10))

CREATE TABLE DATADICT_COLUMN_DESC(DB_ID int,
                                  TABLE_ID int,
                                  COLUMN_ID int,
                                  COLUMN_NAME varchar(30),
                                  COLUMN_DESC varchar(2000))

CREATE TABLE DATADICT_CAVEAT_DESC(DB_ID int,
                                  TABLE_ID int,
                                  CAVEAT_ID int,
                                  CAVEAT_DESC varchar(2000))
```

Let's go over these tables in detail.

First, note that each table listed above contains the column DB_ID. This column is automatically set to the value specified by the variable intDBID within the Visual Basic for Applications (VBA) code. This value **must** be changed for each database for which you want to create a data dictionary in order to keep them separate within the tables shown above. To eliminate the possibility of overwriting what is already stored in the data dictionary tables, create a separate Microsoft Word Data Dictionary Template for each database ensuring the variable intDBID is changed to the next unused value.

The table DATADICT_DB_DEFN will hold the DB_IDs and names for each database for which you are creating a data dictionary. For example, in my template, intDBID is set to 1 and strDBNAME is set to CANDYBAR STUDY DATA. When we talk about how to display the data dictionary in the next chapter, this table will be used to display the names of the databases with data dictionaries available to be viewed. When a new database is created in your company, a new data dictionary template should be created, the variables intDBID and strDBNAME should be filled in appropriately, the template should be filled in itself, and then loaded into the data dictionary tables making the new database available for everyone to view.

The table DATADICT_TABLE_NAME will hold all of the tables found within the completed template. Take note that each table is assigned a unique value under the column TABLE_ID within each DB_ID.   Here, I have limited the length of the table names in the column TABLE_NAME to 30 characters, but you can modify this based on the maximum length of the table names allowable in your database (or across all databases).

The table DATADICT_TABLE_DESC will hold the description of the table itself. Take note that I have limited the table description to 2000 characters, but you can modify this based on the length your desire.   Note that some databases have limits on the number of characters allowed by the VARCHAR (or similar) data type. Please consult with your database administrator and/or the appropriate manuals for your database. (As a guideline, the page you're reading right now contains about 1800 characters in the printed edition.)

The table DATADICT_COLUMN_DEFN will hold the column name, the data type and the nullability of each column within each table. Take note that each column will be assigned a unique value and stored in the column COLUMN_ID. The column COLUMN_NAME will hold the name of the column and is set to 30 characters, but you can modify that based on the maximum length of the column names in your database.

The table DATADICT_COLUMN_DESC will hold the full description of each column and is stored in the column COLUMN_DESC. Take note that I have limited the column description to 2000 characters, but you can modify that based on the length your desire.

The table DATADICT_CAVEAT_DESC will hold the caveats, if any, for each table and will be stored in the column

CAVEAT_DESC. Take note that I have limited the caveat description to 2000 characters, but you can modify that based on the length your desire.

Now, using the appropriate tool, such as Microsoft SQL Server Management Studio, Oracle SQL Developer, Toad, etc., run the appropriate CREATE TABLE statements to create the data dictionary tables on the database that will house the data dictionary tables.

Once completed, modify the Visual Basic form frmPush, shown below, in a similar fashion to how you modified the VB code associated with the Visual Basic form frmPull in a previous chapter.

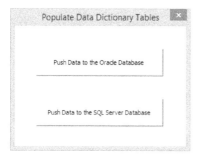

Just as for frmPull, the form frmPush has two buttons, one for Oracle and one for SQL Server. If you're using a different database, add an additional button to the form. Be aware that, despite the two buttons shown in the image above, the data dictionary should probably reside in a *single* database rather than across multiple databases.

Next, double-clicking one of the buttons reveals the VB code that will be executed. For example, double-clicking on the *Push Data to the SQL Server Database* button brings up the following VB code:

```
Private Sub btnPushSQLServer_Click()

'*-----------------------------------------------------------*
'* The line below will execute the UnloadDocumentAndLoadTo-*
```

```
'* SQLServerDB subroutine and populate the data dictionary *
'* tables.                                                  *
'* Make sure to enter in your data source and initial       *
'* catalogue.  Note that data source usually consists of    *
'* the server name which contains a backslash (\).          *
'*---------------------------------------------------------*
 ThisDocument.UnloadDocumentAndLoadToSQLServerDB "ENTER-YOUR-
SERVER-NAME-HERE", "ENTER-YOUR-INITIAL-CATALOGUE-HERE"

End Sub
```

Be sure to enter in your server name as well as the initial catalogue in the code above. For example, I modified the code above to work with my SQL Server database:

```
ThisDocument.UnloadDocumentAndLoadToSQLServerDB "SCOTT-
LAPTOP\SQLEXPRESS","TESTDB"
```

Load the Data Dictionary Tables

Next, let's push the completed template to the database. While in the Visual Basic Editor, double-click frmPush to bring up the form itself, then click F5 (or click the green arrow) to execute the form. The form should appear, as shown in the previous section. Next, click on the appropriate button. For me, I clicked on the *Push Data to the SQL Server Database* button. Note that it may take a while to load the data dictionary tables depending on the number of tables and columns you have in the completed template.

Once completed, you should inspect the data within the database to ensure the load was successful. For example, selecting everything from the DATADICT_TABLE_NAME table, you'll see something similar to the following:

```
DB_ID  TABLE_ID  TABLE_NAME
------ --------- -------------
1      1         CANDYBAR_DIM
1      2         CANDYBAR_FACT
1      3         CANDYMFR_DIM
1      4         DATE_DIM
1      5         RESPONDENT_DIM
```

And for the table DATADICT_COLUMN_DEFN, you'll see something similar to the following (abbreviated output):

```
DB_ID TABLE_ID COLUMN_ID COLUMN_NAME          DATA_TYPE    NULLABILITY
```

```
----- -------- --------- -------------------- ------------ -----------
1     1        1         CANDYBAR_ID          INT          NOT NULL
1     1        2         CANDYBAR_NAME        VARCHAR(50)  NULL
1     1        3         CANDYBAR_MFR_ID      INT          NULL
1     1        4         CANDYBAR_WEIGHT_OZ   FLOAT        NULL
1     2        1         RESPONDENT_ID        INT          NOT NULL
1     2        2         CANDYBAR_ID          INT          NOT NULL
1     2        3         SURVEY_DATE          DATE         NOT NULL
```

And so on for the remaining tables.

One final note is that in order to assign the COLUMN_ID within the table DATADICT_COLUMN_DESC, I had to code a SQL UPDATE statement, shown below:

```
UPDATE DATADICT_COLUMN_DESC
 SET DATADICT_COLUMN_DESC.COLUMN_ID=(SELECT B.COLUMN_ID
  FROM DATADICT_COLUMN_DEFN B
  WHERE DATADICT_COLUMN_DESC.TABLE_ID = B.TABLE_ID
      AND DATADICT_COLUMN_DESC.COLUMN_NAME=B.COLUMN_NAME
      AND DATADICT_COLUMN_DESC.DB_ID=B.DB_ID);
```

Just to be on the safe side, please ensure that that table DATADICT_COLUMN_DESC has the correct COLUMN_IDs in it.

Finally, repeat the process above for each completed template you've created (one for each database). Again, ensure that the intDBID variable is different for each template (database); otherwise, you will overwrite an existing database's data dictionary!

Caution and Warning

Within the Visual Basic for Applications (VBA) code to unload the completed template, there are several things you should be aware of.

First, the Visual Basic code will search for the text *Table Description*, *Column Description* and *Caveats* in order to find the correct section from which to scrape the data. Thus, you should avoid using those words within the descriptions of the tables, columns and caveats. You should also avoid randomly manipulating the template since it's highly sensitive to change unless the VBA has been modified to take the changes into account.

Second, Microsoft Word has an affinity for using fancy apostrophes (i.e., '') and fancy double-quotes (i.e., "") rather than the programmer-approved Courier font apostrophes and double-quotes. Within the code, I replace the fancy double-quotes with normal double-quotes, and the apostrophes with a backtick (i.e., `). You can modify this code as you see fit, just be sure that any ASP.NET or PHP code takes this into account when displaying each table within the browser. Naturally, you don't have to worry about this if you don't use apostrophes or double-quotes within the template.

Third, each section appearing in the Microsoft Word Data Dictionary Template – table name, grid, table description, column bullets and caveats – must appear and cannot be deleted willy-nilly. If you, say, don't have any caveats for a table, enter in one caveat with a description of *None*.

Chapter 5 - *Displaying the Dictionary*

Many Ways to Display the Data Dictionary

In this chapter, we look at several ways to display the data dictionary so your SQL programmers can make best use of it. While there are many ways to display the data dictionary, we'll stick with the following: PHP, ASP.NET, Microsoft SharePoint and MediaWiki. We look into Oracle COMMENTs and SQL Server extended properties in Chapter 8, Data Dictionary Software.

Note that the list of technologies listed above can be broken up into two general categories:

- **Don't** allow users to modify the data dictionary
- **Do** allow users to modify the data dictionary

Technologies such as PHP, ASP.NET, Oracle COMMENTs and SQL Server extended properties are used to display information and the viewers of this information are *generally* prevented from modifying the displayed data, although web programmers and database administrators *could* allow changes.

The remaining technologies, SharePoint and MediaWiki, *generally* permit users to modify wiki pages as well as create new ones, although changes in permissions can disallow this. For example, right now you can go to Wikipedia and make changes to almost any wiki page. As we all know, some people do just this, but not always for the intellectual benefit of mankind. But, there are wiki pages that are locked and can only be changed by someone with the appropriate permission.

So, why am I groaning on about this?

Well, over the last few weeks or months, you've held dictionary content meetings painstakingly defining all of the tables, columns and caveats in one or more databases. Do you really want your programmers, senior or otherwise, to modify your hard work? If you allow your programmers to change the data dictionary, then things are now out of your control. You may be fine with this, but others may not be, especially the stakeholder(s). SharePoint and MediaWiki generally allow for these types of change whereas statically displayed PHP or ASP.NET web pages generally do not.

When my colleagues and I created our data dictionary, we decided to use Active Server Pages (ASP.NET was not available at that time...oh, stop laughing...) to display static web pages. Any changes would need to be requested through the maintainer of the data dictionary. We talk about maintaining the data dictionary in the next chapter.

Naturally, the decision is yours to make.

Although I'm no PHP or ASP.NET expert, I've created some very rudimentary PHP and ASP.NET web pages to give your web programmer a starting point. Be aware, though, that I did not build in a search facility, but your web programmer should. These web pages can then be incorporated into your company's intranet site. You can find these, as well as the Microsoft Word Data Dictionary Template, on my personal website at www.sheepsqueezers.com.

Displaying the Dictionary Using PHP/ASP.NET

Let's look at some of the PHP and ASP.NET code used to display the static web pages.

In both cases, there are only three web pages:

1. CompanyDictionary_DatabaseList.php/.aspx – this page displays the **databases** with associated data dictionaries

2. CompanyDictionary_TableList.php/.aspx – this page displays the list of **tables** for the database selected in #1

3. CompanyDictionary_TableDesc.php/.aspx – this page displays the **table definition** for the table selected in #2

For both PHP and ASP.NET, you will need to connect to the database that houses the data dictionary tables. For example, in my PHP web pages, I connect to the data dictionary tables stored in MySQL like this:

```
//Connect to the database.
$oConn = new mysqli("localhost","scott","tiger","TESTDB");
```

And, for ASP.NET web pages pulling data from a SQL Server database, I connect to the database like this (using C#):

```
//Connect to the database.
String sConn = @"Data Source=SCOTT-LAPTOP\SQLEXPRESS;Initial
Catalog=TESTDB;Integrated Security=SSPI;";
SqlConnection oConn = new SqlConnection(sConn);
oConn.Open();
```

Naturally, this connection code will have to be modified depending in which database you decided to store the data dictionary tables.

Here is the result of requesting the web page CompanyDictionary_Database List.php/.aspx in a browser:

LIST OF AVAILABLE DATABASES	
DATABASE ID	**DATABASE NAME**
1	CANDYBAR STUDY DATA
4	COFFEE STUDY DATA
2	MILK STUDY DATA
3	TEA STUDY DATA

When you click on the CANDYBAR STUDY DATA database link above, you'll be presented with a list of available tables:

LIST OF AVAILABLE TABLES		
TABLE ID	TABLE NAME	TABLE DESCRIPTION
1	CANDYBAR_DIM	Enter description of this table here.
2	CANDYBAR_FACT	Enter description of this table here.
3	CANDYMFR_DIM	Enter description of this table here.
4	DATE_DIM	Enter description of this table here.
5	RESPONDENT_DIM	Enter description of this table here.

Finally, clicking on the table CANDYBAR_FACT table link above, you'll be presented with the definition of the table itself:

Table: CANDYBAR_FACT		
COLUMN NAME	DATABASE DATA TYPE	NULLABILITY
RESPONDENT_ID	INT	NOT NULL
CANDYBAR_ID	INT	NOT NULL
SURVEY_DATE	DATE	NOT NULL
TASTE_RATING	TINYINT	NULL
APPEARANCE_RATING	TINYINT	NULL
TEXTURE_RATING	TINYINT	NULL
OVERALL_RATING	TINYINT	NULL
LIKELIHOOD_PURCHASE	TINYINT	NULL
NBR_BARS_CONSUMED	SMALLINT	NULL

Table Description

Enter description of this table here.

Column Description

- APPEARANCE_RATING: Enter description of this column here.
- CANDYBAR_ID: Enter description of this column here.
- LIKELIHOOD_PURCHASE: Enter description of this column here.
- NBR_BARS_CONSUMED: Enter description of this column here.
- OVERALL_RATING: Enter description of this column here.
- RESPONDENT_ID: Enter description of this column here.
- SURVEY_DATE: Enter description of this column here.
- TASTE_RATING: Enter description of this column here.
- TEXTURE_RATING: Enter description of this column here.

Caveats

- Caveat #1: Enter description of caveat here.

When a search facility is added by your web programmer, looking up which tables contain the column, say, SURVEY_DATE is a snap.

Displaying the Dictionary Using SharePoint

In this section, we talk briefly about how to display the data dictionary within Microsoft SharePoint Foundation 2013.

If you're planning to go the SharePoint route, you'll need to talk with your SharePoint Administrator and request that a site be created to house the data dictionary. For me, I set up a Team Site, but your SharePoint Administrator may suggest a different site type. But, as long as you're able to create wiki pages to hold each table's data dictionary definition, you're good to go. For me, I called my SharePoint Team Site *Company Data Dictionary*, but you should opt for something less generic.

If you completed more than one Microsoft Word Data Dictionary Template, when having a discussion with your SharePoint Administrator mention that you'd like to have one wiki for each database. This will allow you to organize the data dictionary so that tables with the same names, but from different databases, won't be mixed in together. This will go a long way to prevent confusion.

Unfortunately, in order to load each table into a SharePoint wiki page, you'll need to copy the page from the completed Microsoft Word Data Dictionary Template and then paste it into the wiki page. This can be very daunting especially if you have a large number of tables. (It *may* be possible to automate this, so please talk to your SharePoint Administrator first.)

Now, after your SharePoint Administrator has created a Team Site (or other type of site) for you, you'll need to create a wiki for the site. The image below is from SharePoint Foundation 2013, and is the home page screen for my Company Data Dictionary:

Company Data Dictionary   ✎ EDIT LINKS

Company Data Dictionary

Get started with your site   REMOVE THIS

Click on *Add lists, libraries, and other apps.* in order to bring up a list of apps you can add to the site. Below, is a partial list of apps, but take note of the Wiki Page Library icon:

When you click on Wiki Page Library, you'll be asked to name your wiki site, as shown below:

Take note that I entered the name of the database, Candybar Study Data, above. Click on the Create button to create the wiki page library.

When the wiki page library has been created, you'll see it displayed, as shown (in part) below:

On the upper right side of the page, you'll see a tools cog, as shown below.   Clicking that will display the following drop-down box:

Now, in order to add your first wiki **page** to your wiki page **library**, click the Add a page menu item. Similar to naming your wiki page library, you'll be asked to name the wiki page (shown below).

Take note that I am entering in the name of a table from the Candybar Study Data completed template. In this case, I entered CANDYBAR_FACT, as shown above. Click Create to create a blank wiki page for the CANDYBAR_FACT table.

Open up the completed Microsoft Word template, locate the CANDBAR_FACT table, highlight it and copy it to the clipboard. Note that I personally don't highlight the first row containing the table name because SharePoint displays the name of the table automatically when the wiki page is shown in the browser.

When the wiki page is shown, you'll be presented with an empty input box in which to paste the table from the clipboard, as shown below.

Click the Save button to save the wiki page and end the editing session. The completed wiki page will then be displayed, shown (in part) below:

Now, one way to display all of the wiki pages in your wiki library is to click on the Home link, click on the Page link at the top of the page, and click on View All Pages, as shown below:

This is what's displayed when you click on View All Pages:

If you'd like to remove a wiki page, click on the ellipsis to the right of the name of the wiki page and select Delete, as shown below:

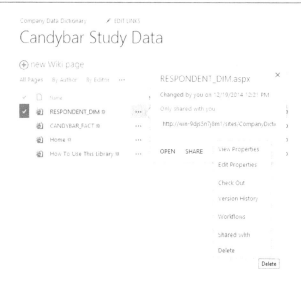

Also, when you're at the Home page for your SharePoint, Team Site, you can add a link to each individual wiki page library by clicking on the Link button on the Insert tab while editing the page itself, as shown below:

Fill in the name to be displayed on the page and then add the address to the wiki page library associated with a particular database, here /sites/CompanyDictionary/Candy bar%20Study%20Data. Clicking OK will add the link to the page, but will not bring you out of edit mode. To exit edit mode, click Save on the Page tab. Here is what you'll see (in part):

Candybar Study Data

Finally, you can search through the entire wiki page library by using the search bar. For example, when searching for the text RESPONDENT_ID, SharePoint returns the following search results:

There's a lot more to SharePoint than what I presented here, so please work with your SharePoint Administrator to enhance your site.

Displaying the Dictionary Using MediaWiki

If you still want to use wiki pages, but don't have Microsoft SharePoint available, you can download the software that runs Wikipedia: MediaWiki. This software can be downloaded from MediaWiki's website at www.mediawiki. org and can be installed on either a Linux or Windows operating system. If you'd like to try it out, you can download TurnKey's Linux MediaWiki Virtual Machine at www. turnkeylinux.org/mediawiki and run it using virtual machine software such as VMWare. The images you see in this section are taken from TurnKey's Linux MediaWiki Virtual Machine.

Unlike with SharePoint, you cannot just copy and paste a table from the Microsoft Word Data Dictionary Template into MediaWiki. This is because MediaWiki uses its own special tags to define tables, bullets, and so on. To ease your pain, you can download and install the *Microsoft Office Word Add-In for MediaWiki* which will allow you to save the Word document in MediaWiki format using the Save As dialog box, shown below:

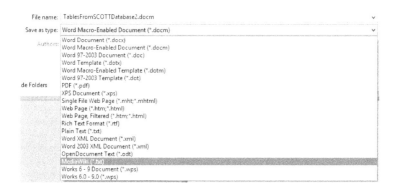

The document will now look like this (only the CANDYBAR_DIM table is shown):

```
{| class="prettytable"
|-
| colspan="3" |
'''Table: CANDYBAR_DIM'''

|-
|
<center>'''COLUMN NAME'''</center>

|
<center>'''DATABASE DATA TYPE'''</center>

|
<center>'''NULLABILITY'''</center>

|-
|
CANDYBAR_ID

|
INT
```

```
|
NOT NULL

|-
|
CANDYBAR_NAME

|
VARCHAR(50)

|
NULL

|-
|
CANDYBAR_MFR_ID

|
INT

|
NULL

|-
|
CANDYBAR_WEIGHT_OZ

|
FLOAT

|
NULL

|}


'''Table Description'''

    Enter description of this table here.

'''Column Description'''

* CANDYBAR_ID: Enter description of this column here.
* CANDYBAR_NAME: Enter description of this column here.
* CANDYBAR_MFR_ID: Enter description of this column here.
* CANDYBAR_WEIGHT_OZ: Enter description of this column here.

'''Caveats'''

* Caveat #1: Enter description of caveat here.
```

It is this text which can be placed in MediaWiki's input box, which we'll shown in just a moment.

First, just like for Wikipedia, to create a new wiki page, type the name of the page in the Search box and click Go. MediaWiki will tell you that the page does not exist, but you will be asked if you want to create it (shown below for the RESPONDENT_DIM table):

Clicking on RESPONDENT DIM above within the text *Create the page "RESPONDENT_DIM" on this wiki!* will start edit mode allowing you to create a wiki page for RESPONDENT_DIM, as shown below:

Next, copy the text generated by the Microsoft Office Word Add-In for MediaWiki for, say, the RESPONDENT_DIM table, paste it into the text box and click the Save Page button at the bottom of the page. You'll then be presented with the results, shown (in part) below:

RESPONDENT DIM

COLUMN NAME	DATABASE DATA TYPE	NULLABILITY
RESPONDENT_ID	INT	NOT NULL
RESPONDENT_NAME	VARCHAR(50)	NULL
RESPONDENT_ADDR	VARCHAR(100)	NULL
RESPONDENT_CITY	VARCHAR(50)	NULL
RESPONDENT_STATE	VARCHAR(2)	NULL
RESPONDENT_ZIPCODE	VARCHAR(9)	NULL
RESPONDENT_PHONE_NUM	VARCHAR(10)	NULL
RESPONDENT_GENDER	VARCHAR(1)	NULL
RESPONDENT_DOB	DATE	NULL

Table Description

Enter description of this table here.

Column Description

▪ RESPONDENT_ID Enter description of this column here
▪ RESPONDENT_NAME Enter description of this column here

Take note that, similar for SharePoint wiki pages, I removed the mention of the table name itself since MediaWiki displays that automatically, as you can see in the image above.

Recall from the last chapter, I mentioned you should create a single wiki page library for each database for which you've created a completed template. This isn't possible for MediaWiki, but you can work around this by adding *categories* to each wiki page. For example, I've added two categories, one indicating that the wiki page is part of the *Company Data Dictionary* category as well as the *Candybar Study Database* category, shown below:

'''Caveats'''

* Caveat #1: Enter description of caveat here.

[[Category:Company Data Dictionary]]
[[Category:Candybar Study Database]]

Please note that all contributions to may be edited, altered, or removed
You are also promising us that you wrote this yourself, or copied it from

You can then easily display all wiki pages associated with a particular category by entering in the text **Category:** followed by the name of the category in the search box. For example, searching for Category:Candybar_Study_Database will return the following results:

Category:Candybar Study Database

There is currently no text in this page. You can search for this page ti

Pages in category "Candybar Study Database"

The following 2 pages are in this category, out of 2 total.

C

- CANDYBAR DIM
- CANDYBAR FACT

Finally, you can retrieve a list of all defined categories by searching for Special:Categories.

Naturally, there's a lot more to MediaWiki than what I just presented, but I hope this gives you a feel for what it can do.

Who Can Access the Data Dictionary?

In Chapter 1, *The Data Dictionary Explained*, I mentioned that my manager was furious that the data dictionary was made public within the organization. While giving everyone in the entire organization access was probably overkill – the security guard probably doesn't need access – there are definitely people who should have access to the data dictionary: database administrators, SQL programmers, data analysts, statisticians, the reference data management group, salespeople, production, and so on. Please have this discussion with your stakeholder(s) before releasing the data dictionary.

Note that access to the data dictionary can be limited by your system administrator, web programmers, SharePoint administrator, MediaWiki administrator, and so on and doesn't necessarily need to be built into the PHP or C# code itself.

Chapter 6 - *Maintaining the Dictionary*

Why Maintain the Data Dictionary?

If it isn't completely obvious, maintaining the data dictionary will allow any new databases, tables and columns to be added as well as any changes to be reflected in the dictionary in a timely fashion, called a *change window*. Let the maintenance of the data dictionary lapse, and you're back to SQL programmers wandering aimlessly around the office muttering the question, "Hey, does anyone know what this table does?"

In this chapter, we focus on who should maintain the data dictionary, how often it needs to be updated, how changes to the dictionary can be requested, and how to be proactive and check for changes yourself.

Who Maintains the Data Dictionary?

You'll probably be surprised I'm not going to automatically nominate one of the database administrators as the maintainer of the data dictionary. While a database administrator is *responsible for* the database, he/she is not necessarily the person who knows the most about the data *contained within* the tables.   And, as I've said before, the data dictionary is all about clear definitions of the tables and columns and the database administrator is probably not your best bet.

In our small company, we have a Reference Data Management (RDM) group whose responsibility is to maintain the small, but all important, dimension tables such as the ICD-9/10 diagnosis codes, the ICD-9/10 procedure codes, the pharmaceutical (NDC) drug codes, and so on. These tables are vital to the organization…without them, no counts, no reports, no data marts, no sales, no nothin'. Is there a similar functionality within your company? If so, then maybe one person within that group should be the maintainer of the data dictionary?

If not, then does your company have a production control group that's responsible for running weekly and/or monthly reports?   If so, then maybe someone within that group should maintain the dictionary.

Regardless whether your company has a reference data management or production control group, choose someone who has a vested interest in the data dictionary. That could be a SQL programmer, a data analyst, and so on. Note that once you find that person, make sure he/she is involved in the data dictionary process from the beginning and is invited to the dictionary content meetings. Also, he/she should be familiar with VBA and SQL.

Frequency of Data Dictionary Updates

The frequency of updates for the data dictionary depends on how fast new production tables are added, modified or deleted as well as how often new production databases are created. The slower these changes are, the less often the dictionary needs to be updated. Faster changes will require more frequent updates. As a general guideline, the data dictionary should be updated at least once a quarter, but you should have a conversation with your database administrator as well as senior SQL programmers to get a feel for how often things change in your organization, if you don't already know yourself.

Requests for Data Dictionary Changes

No matter how diligent you've been describing the tables, columns and caveats during the dictionary content meetings, changes must be made to the data dictionary in order to keep it *au courant*. Any desired changes to be made to the data dictionary should be requested through the maintainer of the data dictionary as well as the people invited to the dictionary content meetings. The maintainer should **not** automatically change the dictionary without the change(s) being vetted.

Some organizations may want to have meetings, akin to dictionary content meetings, to discuss these changes. At these meetings, requested changes can be accepted, declined or modified.

For example, when I worked at a large pharmaceutical company, I requested that the length of a certain character field be increased to accommodate larger descriptions. A meeting was held and I was granted *two additional characters*. My e-mail response, stating my overwhelming gratitude for this change, was formed using only two characters per line.

Note that some changes may need to be made outside of the normal change window (quarterly, as mentioned in the previous section) if there's an egregious mistake in a table or column description or caveat.

Naturally, if you're using SharePoint or MediaWiki and are allowing anyone to make changes to the data dictionary at any time, then the above discussion is moot…which is why I don't recommend SharePoint or MediaWiki without some change control being enforced. Please talk with your SharePoint or MediaWiki administrator for more information.

Be a Proactive Superhero!

No matter how diligent everyone is at maintaining the data dictionary, occasionally a change to the database will be made and that change will not be reflected in the data dictionary. This could happen if a database administrator adds a new column or changes a data type of an existing column and forgets to tell you about it. These things will happen, so there's no use saber rattling over them. But, you can occasionally check for changes like this by running a SQL query comparing the data dictionary's contents against the database's internal dictionary. If you find a mismatch, then the data dictionary needs to be modified.

Below, we show SQL code in Oracle, but similar SQL can be created in your database. First, let's check for changes to the tables. Using the data dictionary table DATADICT_ TABLE_NAME, let's comparing it against the system view ALL_TABLES:

```
SELECT CASE
       WHEN A.TABLE_NAME IS NOT NULL
            AND B.TABLE_NAME IS NULL THEN '*****NEW*****'
       WHEN A.TABLE_NAME IS NULL
            AND B.TABLE_NAME IS NOT NULL THEN '*****DEL*****'
       WHEN A.TABLE_NAME IS NOT NULL
            AND B.TABLE_NAME IS NOT NULL THEN '*****BOTH****'
       END AS ACTION,
       A.TABLE_NAME AS ORACLE_TABLE_NAME,
       B.TABLE_NAME AS DICT_TABLE_NAME
 FROM ALL_TABLES A FULL OUTER JOIN DATADICT_TABLE_NAME B
ON A.TABLE_NAME=B.TABLE_NAME
WHERE A.OWNER IS NULL
       OR A.OWNER='SCOTT'
ORDER BY 1,2;
```

Here are the results of this query when run subsetting for tables owned by SCOTT:

ACTION	ORACLE TABLE NAME	DICT TABLE NAME
*****BOTH****	CANDYBAR_DIM	CANDYBAR_DIM
*****BOTH****	CANDYBAR_FACT	CANDYBAR_FACT
*****BOTH****	RESPONDENT_DIM	RESPONDENT_DIM
*****DEL*****		CANDYMFR_DIM
*****DEL*****		DATE_DIM
*****NEW*****	CHILDSTATBMI	
*****NEW*****	COUNTRYCODES	

As you can see above, three of the tables appear in the data dictionary as well as in the system view ALL_TABLES, as indicated by BOTH under the column ACTION. No action is require for these tables unless there have been changes to any of their columns (see below).

Two tables are new and do not appear in the data dictionary, CHILDSTATBMI and COUNTRYCODES, as indicated by NEW under the column ACTION. These two tables need to be added to the data dictionary.

Two tables appearing in the data dictionary have been removed from the database, as indicated by DEL under the column ACTION. Instead of removing these tables from the data dictionary, their table descriptions should be modified to indicate that they've been deprecated.

Note that the column OWNER for the two tables CANDYMFR_DIM and DATE_DIM will be NULL which is why this is being tested for in the WHERE Clause above.

Next, you can do a similar thing to check for additions and/or deletions of columns as well as changes to the data types and nullability. In Oracle, the system view ALL_TAB_COLUMNS can be compared against the data dictionary table DATADICT_COLUMN_DEFN:

```
SELECT CASE
        WHEN A.COLUMN_NAME IS NOT NULL
            AND B.COLUMN_NAME IS NULL THEN '*****NEW*****'
        WHEN A.COLUMN_NAME IS NULL
            AND B.COLUMN_NAME IS NOT NULL THEN '*****DEL*****'
        WHEN A.COLUMN_NAME IS NOT NULL
            AND B.COLUMN_NAME IS NOT NULL THEN '*****BOTH****'
        END AS ACTION,
        A.TABLE_NAME AS ORACLE_TABLE_NAME,
        A.COLUMN_NAME AS ORACLE_COLUMN_NAME,
        B.TABLE_NAME AS DICT_TABLE_NAME,
        B.COLUMN_NAME AS DICT_COLUMN_NAME
  FROM ALL_TAB_COLUMNS A FULL OUTER JOIN (
    SELECT Y.TABLE_NAME,X.COLUMN_NAME
    FROM DATADICT_COLUMN_DEFN X INNER JOIN DATADICT_TABLE_NAME Y
    ON X.DB_ID=Y.DB_ID
        AND X.TABLE_ID=Y.TABLE_ID) B
  ON A.TABLE_NAME=B.TABLE_NAME
    AND A.COLUMN_NAME=B.COLUMN_NAME
WHERE A.OWNER IS NULL
        OR A.OWNER='SCOTT'
    ORDER BY 1,2;
```

ACTION	ORACLE TABLE NAME	ORACLE COLUMN NAME	DICT TABLE NAME	DICT COLUMN NAME
*****BOTH****	CANDYBAR_DIM	CANDYBAR_ID	CANDYBAR_DIM	CANDYBAR_ID
*****BOTH****	CANDYBAR_DIM	CANDYBAR_NAME	CANDYBAR_DIM	CANDYBAR_NAME
*****BOTH****	CANDYBAR_DIM	CANDYBAR_WEIGHT_OZ	CANDYBAR_DIM	CANDYBAR_WEIGHT_OZ
*****BOTH****	CANDYBAR_FACT	NBR_BARS_CONSUMED	CANDYBAR_FACT	NBR_BARS_CONSUMED
*****BOTH****	CANDYBAR_FACT	OVERALL_RATING	CANDYBAR_FACT	OVERALL_RATING
*****BOTH****	CANDYBAR_FACT	SURVEY_DATE	CANDYBAR_FACT	SURVEY_DATE
*****BOTH****	CANDYBAR_FACT	RESPONDENT_ID	CANDYBAR_FACT	RESPONDENT_ID
*****BOTH****	CANDYBAR_FACT	CANDYBAR_ID	CANDYBAR_FACT	CANDYBAR_ID
*****BOTH****	RESPONDENT_DIM	RESPONDENT_CITY	RESPONDENT_DIM	RESPONDENT_CITY
*****BOTH****	RESPONDENT_DIM	RESPONDENT_STATE	RESPONDENT_DIM	RESPONDENT_STATE
*****BOTH****	RESPONDENT_DIM	RESPONDENT_ZIPCODE	RESPONDENT_DIM	RESPONDENT_ZIPCODE
*****BOTH****	RESPONDENT_DIM	RESPONDENT_PHONE_NUM	RESPONDENT_DIM	RESPONDENT_PHONE_NUM
*****BOTH****	RESPONDENT_DIM	RESPONDENT_ADDR	RESPONDENT_DIM	RESPONDENT_ADDR
*****BOTH****	RESPONDENT_DIM	RESPONDENT_DOB	RESPONDENT_DIM	RESPONDENT_DOB
*****BOTH****	RESPONDENT_DIM	RESPONDENT_NAME	RESPONDENT_DIM	RESPONDENT_NAME

```
*****BOTH**** RESPONDENT_DIM    RESPONDENT_ID          RESPONDENT_DIM  RESPONDENT_ID
*****BOTH**** RESPONDENT_DIM    RESPONDENT_GENDER      RESPONDENT_DIM  RESPONDENT_GENDER
*****DEL*****                                          CANDYBAR_FACT   APPEARANCE_RATING
*****DEL*****                                          CANDYBAR_FACT   LIKELIHOOD_PURCHASE
*****DEL*****                                          CANDYBAR_DIM    CANDYBAR_MFR_ID
*****DEL*****                                          CANDYMFR_DIM    CANDYBAR_MFR_NAME
*****NEW***** CHILDSTATBMI      BMI
*****NEW***** CHILDSTATBMI      FIRSTNAME
*****NEW***** CHILDSTATBMI      GENDER
*****NEW***** CHILDSTATBMI      BIRTHDATE
*****NEW***** CHILDSTATBMI      HEIGHT
*****NEW***** CHILDSTATBMI      WEIGHT
*****NEW***** COUNTRYCODES      COUNTRY_NAME
*****NEW***** COUNTRYCODES      COUNTRY
```

Notice that for the tables CANDYBAR_FACT and CANDYBAR_DIM, several columns appear in the data dictionary which no longer appear in the database tables, as indicated by the DEL under the column ACTION. You can either remove these columns from the data dictionary, or you can change their descriptions to include the word DEPRECATED.

Notice that several new columns appear, as indicated by NEW under the column ACTION. These just happen to be the columns for the two new tables CHILDSTATBMI and COUNTRYCODES. Once these new tables are added to the dictionary, these columns will be indicated as BOTH under the column ACTION above.

To check for data type and nullability changes, you can issue the following SQL code:

```
SELECT CASE
         WHEN A.DATTYP=B.DATA_TYPE THEN '*****MATCH*****'
         ELSE '*****MIS-MATCH*****'
       END AS DATA_TYPE_ACTION,
       CASE
         WHEN A.NULLRES=B.NULLABILITY THEN '*****MATCH*****'
         ELSE '*****MIS-MATCH*****'
       END AS NULLABILITY_ACTION,
       A.TABLE_NAME AS ORACLE_TABLE_NAME,
       A.COLUMN_NAME AS ORACLE_COLUMN_NAME,
       A.DATTYP AS ORACLE_DATA_TYPE,
       A.NULLRES AS ORACLE_NULLABILITY,
       B.TABLE_NAME AS DICT_TABLE_NAME,
       B.COLUMN_NAME AS DICT_COLUMN_NAME,
       B.DATA_TYPE AS DICT_DATA_TYPE,
       B.NULLABILITY AS DICT_NULLABILITY
 FROM (
       SELECT TABLE_NAME,COLUMN_NAME,
       CASE
         WHEN DATA_TYPE='DATE' THEN 'DATE'
         WHEN DATA_TYPE='VARCHAR2'
```

```
        THEN 'VARCHAR2(' || TO_CHAR(DATA_LENGTH) || ')'
   WHEN DATA_TYPE='NUMBER' AND DATA_PRECISION IS NOT NULL
        THEN 'NUMBER(' || TO_CHAR(DATA_PRECISION)
                  || ',' || TO_CHAR(DATA_SCALE) || ')'
   WHEN DATA_TYPE='NUMBER' AND DATA_PRECISION IS NULL
        THEN 'NUMBER'
   WHEN DATA_TYPE='BLOB' THEN 'BLOB'
   WHEN DATA_TYPE='ROWID' THEN 'ROWID'
   WHEN DATA_TYPE='CHAR'
        THEN 'CHAR(' || TO_CHAR(DATA_LENGTH) || ')'
   ELSE 'UNKNOWN'
   END AS DATTYP,
   CASE
    WHEN NULLABLE='N' THEN 'NOT NULL'
    WHEN NULLABLE='Y' THEN 'NULL'
    ELSE 'NULL?'
   END AS NULLRES
   FROM ALL_TAB_COLUMNS
   WHERE OWNER='SCOTT'
  ) A
 FULL OUTER JOIN
 (
  SELECT Y.TABLE_NAME,X.COLUMN_NAME,
         X.DATA_TYPE,X.NULLABILITY
   FROM DATADICT_COLUMN_DEFN X
        INNER JOIN DATADICT_TABLE_NAME Y
   ON X.DB_ID=Y.DB_ID
      AND X.TABLE_ID=Y.TABLE_ID
 ) B
ON A.TABLE_NAME=B.TABLE_NAME
   AND A.COLUMN_NAME=B.COLUMN_NAME
ORDER BY 1,2;
```

Feel free to modify the SQL code shown throughout this section to limit the results to just the new and changed items.

Finally, if you've populated several Microsoft Word Data Dictionary Templates from different databases – such as Oracle, SQL Server, Teradata, MySQL, etc. – then you will have to either modify/run the SQL above on those systems or connect to the other databases from within a central database.

So...How Do I Modify the Data Dictionary?

In this section, I outline how to safely make modifications to the data dictionary. As we discussed in the previous section, there are several types of modifications you can make to the data dictionary:

1. Add an additional table

2. Add an additional column
3. Add an additional caveat
4. Modify a column's data type
5. Modify a column's nullability
6. Modify a caveat
7. Remove a table
8. Remove a column
9. Remove a caveat

For #7, *Remove a table*, I already mentioned that you probably don't want to remove a table from the data dictionary, but place the word DEPRECATED at the beginning of the table's description.

For #8, *Remove a column*, you can either remove the column or include the word DEPRECATED in the column's description. If you decide to remove the column, remove the column's row within the grid as well as the column name and description from the column description section.

For #9, *Remove a caveat*, you can remove the caveat directly in the completed Microsoft Word Data Dictionary Template by removing it from the caveat section. But, remember that at least one caveat must appear, even if it contains the description *None*.

For #4, *Modify a column's data type*, #5, *Modify a column's nullability* and #6, *Modify a caveat*, you can make these modifications directly within the completed Microsoft Word Data Dictionary Template itself.

For #2, *Add an additional column*, you can simply extend the grid associated with the table, adding in the column's name, data type and nullability as well as add the column within the column description section as an additional bullet point.

For #3, *Add an additional caveat*, you can simply add another bullet point in the caveats section in the completed Microsoft Word Data Dictionary Template.

For #1, *Add an additional table*, there are two ways to do this. First, if you only have one or two new tables to deal with, you can just cut-and-paste an existing table within the completed Microsoft Word Data Dictionary Template and then modify it to contain the new table name, columns, data types, nullability and caveats. Second, you can create a new blank template based on my Microsoft Word Data Dictionary Template, pull in only those new tables by modifying the SQL code as outlined in Chapter 2, *The Data Dictionary and Microsoft Word*, and copy these tables and paste them into the completed Microsoft Word Data Dictionary Template.

Naturally, you will need to reload the completed template (additions, modifications, deletions, and all) back into the data dictionary tables, as outlined in Chapter 4, *Loading the Dictionary Into the Database*.

Note that if you've gone the SharePoint or MediaWiki route, you'll have to enter these in by hand via that software's interface.

A Comment on the Data Dictionary Tables

In Chapter 4, *Loading the Dictionary Into the Database*, we talked about how to load the information contained within a completed Microsoft Word Data Dictionary Template for a specific database's tables into several database tables such as DATADICT_TABLE_NAME, DATADICT_COLUMN_ DEFN and so on. In this section, I'd like to talk about how to ensure that these tables remain safe from any modifications as outlined in the previous section. This section only pertains to you if you've decided to display the dictionary using PHP, ASP.NET or similar, and can be ignored if you've gone the SharePoint or MediaWiki route.

One way to handle changing tables is to have your database administrator create three schemas for you to work with: development, test and production. These schemas will all contain the data dictionary tables, but only the tables contained within the **production** schema will be used to source your company's live data dictionary via PHP, ASP.NET, etc.

The **test** schema will contain any changes you've made to the data dictionary tables and will be the source for the test version of the company's data dictionary website. This way, any problems can be found immediately before copying the test schema's tables over to the production schema. Naturally, this assumes that your web programmer has created a separate test website for you for verification purposes. If you're happy with the changes in the test schema, then you can copy the tables over to the production schema.

Finally, the **development** schema is used solely for you to play with and test out new ideas. If you're happy with the changes made to the data dictionary tables within the development schema you can then copy them over to the test schema.

It's by dividing up the data dictionary into these three schemas that affords you some comfort that any changes made will not make it into the production schema unless you're completely happy with those changes.

You may also want to ask your database administrator if the data dictionary tables are part of the normal backup process. If not, he/she should be able to add them in fairly quickly.

A Comment on SharePoint and MediaWiki

In the previous section, I showed you my innate medically-controlled paranoia by indicating that the data dictionary tables should be loaded into a development, a test and a production schema. The previous section assumed that you are displaying the dictionary using PHP, ASP.NET, or similar. In this section, let's talk about SharePoint and MediaWiki.

When using SharePoint, your SharePoint administrator most likely chose to use Microsoft SQL Server as the data store. Please have a conversation with your SharePoint administrator asking if backups are performed on the database specifically for the SharePoint data. If not, you may want to ask if this can be done. It would be ashamed to load the entire data dictionary into wikis only to have the data lost due to a disk failure or stray gamma particle.

A similar comment goes for MediaWiki. Please talk to your MediaWiki administrator about his/her process for backing up the data store behind the software.

A Comment on the Completed Templates

While we're discussing safety and security, please ensure that all of your completed data dictionary templates are stored safely in your company's revision/version control software such as Git, Subversion, Mercurial, and so on.

Note that some revision control programs allow for special tags to be entered directly into the code itself. For example, tags such as the current date and time, the name of the file itself, and so on. These tags are replaced when the code is *checked out* via the revision control's interface and are fine for text files, but they should **never** be placed into a Microsoft Word document, especially older versions of Word. Never versions of Word (.docx) are just compressed (zipped) XML files and should work fine with these revision control tags…but I wouldn't take a chance.

Now, if you'll excuse me, I have to take more anti-paranoia medication.

Chapter 7 - *Extending the Data Dictionary*

Functions and Procedures

Although having table and column descriptions, data types, nullability as well as caveats available on your intranet's webby-web, other objects such as functions and procedures should probably appear in the data dictionary as well. In this section, we show you how to modify the Microsoft Word Data Dictionary Template to include functions and procedures as well as their parameters and data types.

Knowing that not everyone reading this book will have home-grown user-defined functions and procedures lurking in their databases, I've created a separate template which focuses specifically on functions and procedures. **This template should contain the same intDBID as that of the corresponding data dictionary template's intDBID.** Also, several new data dictionary tables need to be created to accommodate the function, procedure and parameter descriptions. The template is called the *Microsoft Word Data Dictionary Functions and Procedures Template* and is available on my personal website sheepsqueezers.com.

Similar to the Microsoft Word Data Dictionary Template, the Microsoft Word Functions and Procedures Template contains several subroutines used to initially populate the template. These subroutines are PullOracleFunctionsAnd Procedures and PullSQLServerFunctionsAndProcedures.

Once the template has been populated, you should fill in the function and procedure descriptions, describe the arguments and return type (if any), and mention any caveats for the functions and procedures.

Note that the subroutine PullOracleFunctionsAndProcedures ignores those functions and procedures stored within a package. Please modify the SQL code to pull in package information if you have home-grown packages.

The following additional tables need to be added alongside the data dictionary tables created in Chapter 4, *Loading the Dictionary into the Database*.

```
CREATE TABLE DATADICT_FUNCPROC_NAME(DB_ID int,
                                    FUNCPROC_ID int,
                                    FUNCPROC_TYPE varchar(1),
                                    FUNCPROC_NAME varchar(30))

CREATE TABLE DATADICT_FUNCPROC_DESC(DB_ID int,
                                    FUNCPROC_ID int,
                                    FUNCPROC_DESC varchar(2000))

CREATE TABLE DATADICT_FUNCPROCCAVEAT_DESC(DB_ID int,
                                    FUNCPROC_ID int,
                                    CAVEAT_ID int,
                                    CAVEAT_DESC varchar(2000))

CREATE TABLE DATADICT_ARGUMENT_DESC(DB_ID int,
                                    FUNCPROC_ID int,
                                    ARGUMENT_ID int,
                                    ARGUMENT_NAME varchar(30),
                                    ARGUMENT_DESC varchar(2000))

CREATE TABLE DATADICT_ARGUMENT_DEFN(DB_ID int,
                                    FUNCPROC_ID int,
                                    ARGUMENT_ID int,
                                    ARGUMENT_NAME varchar(30),
                                    DIRECTION varchar(6),
                                    DATATYPE varchar(10))
```

These tables are in a similar format to their data dictionary cousins with each table containing the column DB_ID which maps to the intDBID within the Visual Basic for Applications (VBA) code.

The tables DATADICT_FUNCPROC_NAME and DATADICT _FUNCPROC_DESC contain the name and description for each function and procedure listed in the Microsoft Word Functions and Procedures Template. Note that the column FUNCPROC_TYPE is set to "F" for a function and "P" for a procedure.

The tables DATADICT_ARGUMENT_DESC and DATA DICT_ARGUMENT_DEFN describe the arguments, if any, for the functions and procedures as well as the direction of the argument (IN or OUT) as well as the argument's data type.

Finally, the table DATADICT_FUNCPROCCAVEAT_DESC contains the caveats for each function and procedure.

When you've finished creating these new tables, you can run the appropriate load subroutine using the appropriate form. The unload subroutines are UnloadDocumentAnd LoadToOracleDB and UnloadDocumentAndLoadToSQL ServerDB.

If you are using neither SQL Server nor Oracle, please create a load and unload routine for your database using its metadata tables.

Finally, I've created additional rudimentary PHP and ASP.NET web pages to display the data contains within these tables. Please see CompanyDictionary_DatabaseList .php/.aspx, CompanyDictionary_FuncProcList.php/.aspx and CompanyDictionary_FuncProcDesc.php/.aspx. Your web programmer should incorporate these files into your intranet site along with the data dictionary web pages.

And, of course, you can find these files along with the other files mentioned throughout the book on my personal website at www.sheepsqueezers.com.

Business Logic

Business Logic, according to Wikipedia, defines how data is transformed or computed for use with your software. Business Logic is sometimes referred to as Business Rules (although Wikipedia distinguishes the two).

For example, given the column RESPONDENT_GENDER, business logic would dictate what to do with values that are neither male nor female. Business logic would outline, say, how to compute the column GrossProfit based on the columns TotalRevenue and TotalCost.

Although I haven't built them into the templates, you may want to think about either adding a section for business logic as part of each table in the Microsoft Word Data Dictionary Template itself, or as a completely separate template dedicated to business logic.

For example, here's an example section containing business logic that can be very easily added to the template:

Business Logic

- BL.1 - The column RESPONDENT_GENDER should be transformed to take on only the values Male, Female and Unknown. NULL values are to be coded as Unknown.
- BL.2 - The column GrossProfit is computed as TotalRevenue minus TotalCost. If either TotalRevenue or TotalCost contains a NULL value, GrossProfit should be set to NULL.

The VBA code for the caveats section can be used with business logic.

Code Examples

Another helpful section to add to the data dictionary is code examples. Just like for business logic, you can add an additional section to the Microsoft Word Data Dictionary Template. For example,

Code Examples

- SQL Code to bring the RESPONDENT_GENDER column in line with BL.1:

```
CASE
 WHEN RESPONDENT_GENDER IN ('M','F')
                          THEN RESPONDENT_GENDER
 ELSE 'OTHER'
END AS RESPONDENT_GENDER_BR1
```

- To executing the INSERT_COUNTRY stored procedure, run code similar to the following:

```
EXEC INSERT_COUNTRY "US","United States"
```

You can then save the code examples to the database as a text string, but be aware that some databases allow you to work with XML, so you may want to save each code example as an XML CDATA section. Please talk to your database administrator for more information.

In any case, since handling code fragments is more difficult than business logic discussed above, I created an additional template, called Microsoft Word Data Dictionary CODE FRAGMENT Template and placed it along with all of the other downloads for this book on my personal website sheepsqueezers.com. Use this template if you want to include code fragments in the data dictionary.

A word of caution: the Code Examples section MUST appear for each table in this template even if you have no code examples to show. In this case, the bullet should contain the text *No code examples:* and the single line of code can be set to *None*.

Note that the two **unload** routines in this template have been modified, but the two **load** routines have not. You can either modify the load routines or just copy the Code Examples section into the populated template yourself and modify it as you see fit.

Chapter 8 – *Data Dictionary Software*

Introduction

In this chapter, we take a look at some of the free and not-so-free software out there that can maintain data dictionaries as well as generate dictionary-related documentation. But, before diving into the software itself, we talk about Oracle's COMMENT statement, SQL Server's extended properties and how to capture comments during the database design phase using software such as CA Technologies' ERwin Data Modeler.

Using Oracle COMMENTs

Yes, Silly-Billy, you *can* associate comments with tables and columns in Oracle…it's just not used that often, sadly.

To associate a comment with a table, you use the following code:

```
COMMENT ON TABLE table-name IS 'descriptive text';
```

For example, let's place a comment on the CANDBAR_DIM table:

```
COMMENT ON TABLE CANDYBAR_DIM IS 'This table contains a list of candybars used in the Candybar Study.';
```

To associate a comment with a column of a table, you use the following code:

```
COMMENT ON COLUMN table-name.column-name IS 'descriptive text';
```

For example, let's place a comment on the column CANDYBAR_ID within the CANDYBAR_DIM table:

```
COMMENT ON COLUMN CANDYBAR_DIM.CANDYBAR_ID IS 'This
column contains the identifier for each candybar and
contains values such as 1, 2, 3, and so on.';
```

Now, table and column comments are stored in the following two database dictionary views:

- ALL_TAB_COMMENTS

```
Name       Null      Type
---------- -------- --------------
OWNER        NOT NULL VARCHAR2(128)
TABLE_NAME NOT NULL VARCHAR2(128)
TABLE_TYPE          VARCHAR2(11)
COMMENTS           VARCHAR2(4000)
```

- ALL_COL_COMMENTS

```
Name        Null      Type
----------- -------- --------------
OWNER         NOT NULL VARCHAR2(128)
TABLE_NAME  NOT NULL VARCHAR2(128)
COLUMN_NAME NOT NULL VARCHAR2(128)
COMMENTS            VARCHAR2(4000)
```

For example, to retrieve the table comment created from the SQL code above, you can code something like this:

```
SELECT COMMENTS
 FROM ALL_TAB_COMMENTS
 WHERE OWNER='SCOTT'
      AND TABLE_NAME='CANDYBAR_DIM';

COMMENTS
----------------------------------------------------
This table contains a list of candybars used in the
Candybar Study.
```

And similar for the column comment:

```
SELECT COMMENTS
 FROM ALL_COL_COMMENTS
 WHERE OWNER='SCOTT'
      AND TABLE_NAME='CANDYBAR_DIM'
      AND COLUMN_NAME='CANDYBAR_ID';

COMMENTS
----------------------------------------------------
This column contains the identifier for each candybar
and contains values such as 1, 2, 3, and so on.
```

Before generating the populated Microsoft Word Data Dictionary template for any database, please ask your Oracle database administrator if comments have been created for, as well as maintained within, the database. If so, you can modify the SQL query described in Chapter 2, *The Data Dictionary and Microsoft Word* to include the available comments within ALL_TAB_COMMENTS and ALL_COL_ COMMENTS to pre-populate the template.

Note that even if comments are available, dictionary content meetings are still useful since these comments may not be descriptive enough for use by new hires, salespeople, data analysts, statisticians, and so on.

For those of you who use Oracle SQL Developer, you can view and add comments via the GUI rather than by SQL code. We show examples of Oracle SQL Developer below, but please check your GUI (e.g.,Toad, Allround Automations' PL/SQL Developer, etc.) for similar functionality.

Open up Oracle SQL Developer and expand the Tables folder under your database's connection. To enter a comment for a table, right-click on the name of the table, then click on Comment... under the Table menu item, shown below.

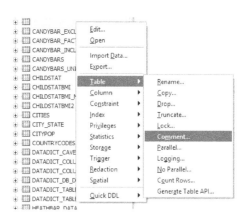

The Comment dialog box, as shown below, will be displayed. In the input box to the right of the word Comment, enter in your description of the table.

By clicking on the SQL tab, you can see the Oracle COMMENT SQL code, shown below.

Click Apply to save the comment.

To enter a comment for a column, right-click on the name of the table, then click on Comment... under the Column menu item, shown below.

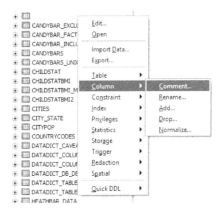

In this case, though, the Comment dialog box includes a Column selection drop-down box, shown below.

Select the column on which you want to create a comment, then fill in the comment in the Comment input box. Note that this dialog box will allow you to create comments on each column. For example, below I'm creating a comment on the column CANDYBAR_ID.

Click Apply to apply these comments to each of the columns.

Alternatively, you can display the Comment dialog box for a specific column by clicking on the Comment… menu item after right-clicking the desired column under the table, shown below.

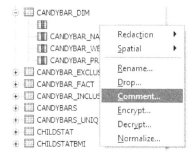

Using SQL Server Extended Properties

SQL Server allows you to make comments similar to that of Oracle either via SQL Server Management Studio's GUI or by SQL code. First, let's look at the GUI interface.

Comments are placed in the Extended Properties portion of the GUI interface either for a table or for one or more columns within a table. You can bring up the Table

Properties dialog box by right-clicking on the table name and clicking the Properties menu item, shown below.

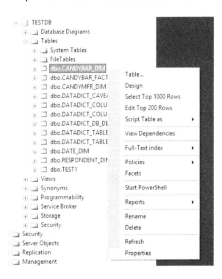

By clicking on the Extended Properties item in the *Select a page* pane on the left side of the dialog box, the table's extended properties will be displayed, shown below.

Now, extended properties are in the form of a name-value pair. For example, for the table CANDYBAR_DIM, I set the **name** to *Description* and the **value** to *This table contains a list of candybars used in the Candybar Study.* in the dialog box shown above. Click OK to dismiss the dialog box.

Note that we can add additional name-value pairs for, say, caveats, shown below.

You can create name-value pairs for columns as well. In this case, click on the Properties menu item for the column on which you want to make a comment, shown below.

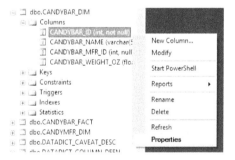

Note that table and column extended properties are stored in the database separately, so don't be afraid of using the word *Description* for both table and column name-value pairs.

You can also create extended properties for functions and stored procedures. But, be aware that parameters and return values do not have a Properties menu item, so Extended

Properties are not visible through SQL Server Management Studio's interface. With that said, you can add extended properties using the sp_addextendedproperty, as described below.

Now, you can retrieve these extended properties by using the SQL function fn_listextendedproperty. For example, to retrieve the name-value pairs for the table CANDYBAR_DIM, you can use the following code:

```
SELECT objname AS table_name,name,value
 FROM fn_listextendedproperty(NULL,
                               'SCHEMA','dbo',
                               'TABLE','CANDYBAR_DIM',
                               NULL,NULL);
```

The first parameter allows you to select a specific extended property by name within quotes. Here we set it to NULL to pull in all extended properties. The third parameter specifies the schema dbo. The second parameter indicates that the third parameter contains a schema name. The fifth parameter specifies the table whose extended properties you want, CANDYBAR_DIM. The fourth parameter indicates that the fifth parameter contains a table name. The last two parameters are used when pulling a column's extended properties, and we'll see that in just a moment.

And, here are the results:

	table_name	name	value
1	CANDYBAR_DIM	Caveat_1	This is a dangerous table!
2	CANDYBAR_DIM	Caveat_2	This is a very dangerous table!
3	CANDYBAR_DIM	Description	This table contains a list of candybars used in the Candybar Study

If you'd like a specific extended property, specify it in the first parameter:

```
SELECT objname AS table_name,name,value
 FROM fn_listextendedproperty('Description',
                               'SCHEMA','dbo',
                               'TABLE','CANDYBAR_DIM',
                               NULL,NULL);
```

Results   Messages

	table_name	name	value
1	CANDYBAR_DIM	Description	This table contains a list of candybars used in the Candybar Study.

Alternatively, you can use a WHERE Clause specifying the properties you want using the name column:

```
SELECT objname AS table_name,name,value
 FROM fn_listextendedproperty(NULL,
                              'SCHEMA','dbo',
                              'TABLE','CANDYBAR_DIM',
                              NULL,NULL)
 WHERE name IN ('Caveat_1','Caveat_2');
```

Results   Messages

	table_name	name	value
1	CANDYBAR_DIM	Caveat_1	This is a dangerous table!
2	CANDYBAR_DIM	Caveat_2	This is a very dangerous table!

To pull all of the name-value pairs for a specific column, you can use code similar to that shown above by specifying 'COLUMN' in the sixth parameter and the name of the column in the seventh parameter:

```
SELECT objname AS table_name,name,value
 FROM fn_listextendedproperty(NULL,
                              'SCHEMA','dbo',
                              'TABLE','CANDYBAR_DIM',
                              'COLUMN','CANDYBAR_ID');
```

Results   Messages

	table_name	name	value
1	CANDYBAR_ID	Description	This column contains the identifier for each candybar and contains values such as 1, 2, 3, and so on.

Now, if you would prefer to add, update or remove extended properties using SQL code, you can make use of the stored procedures sp_addextendedproperty, sp_updateextended property, and sp_dropextendedproperty.

For example, to add a third caveat, 'Caveat_3', to the table's existing extended properties, you can code something like this:

```
EXEC sp_addextendedproperty 'Caveat_3','DANGER!!',
                             'SCHEMA','dbo',
                             'TABLE','CANDYBAR_DIM';
```

The first parameter is the name of the extended property,
followed by the value of extended property in the second
parameter.   The remaining parameters are similar to the
function fn_listextendedproperty described above. Here's
what the table's extended properties page looks like in the
GUI now:

As described, you cannot add extended properties to a
parameter via the GUI interface, but you can add an
extended property to a parameter using sp_addextended
property. For example, here we're adding a comment to the
@NUM1 parameter of the ADD_ONE function:

```
EXEC sp_addextendedproperty 'MS_Description','BOINK!',
                            'SCHEMA','dbo',
                            'FUNCTION', 'ADD_ONE',
                            'PARAMETER', '@NUM1'
```

Please see Microsoft's website for more on these stored procedures and functions.

Wait…Can this be done at design time?

When designing a database, you don't have to limit yourself to a piece of paper and a pencil. Several elaborate – and bloody expensive! – pieces of software are available specifically for designing databases such as CA Technologies' ERwin Data Modeler, Embarcadero's ER/Studio and Toad Data Modeler. Specific to the topic of this book, these products allow you to specify table and column comments that will be generated when the database design is forward engineered to the target database. For Oracle, a series of COMMENTs are generated. For SQL Server, a series of sp_addextendedproperty stored procedures are generated.

Let's use CA Technologies' ERwin Data Modeler to design a single table, CANDYBAR_DIM. We will then add table and column comments and then take a look at what ERwin generates for SQL Server and for Oracle.

Note that I selected the target database by clicking on Actions…Target Database… In the text that follows, I create one ERwin diagram setting SQL Server as the target database, and another setting Oracle as the target database.

After adding a table object to the blank model, adding columns, data types and nullability, here's what the design of this table looks like, at least as far as SQL Server is concerned:

CANDYBAR_DIM

CANDYBAR_ID: int NOT NULL

CANDYBAR_NAME: varchar(50) NULL
CANDYBAR_MFR_ID: int NULL
CANDYBAR_WEIGHT_OZ: float NULL

Now, to add a comment to the *table* itself, right-click on the object CANDYBAR_DIM and click the Table Properties... menu item, shown below.

When the editor appears, click on the Comment tab, and type your comment in the input box provided, shown below. **Make sure to select the schema, here set to dbo, under the column labeled Schema.**

Click the Close button to save your comment and dismiss the editor.

To make comments on one or more *columns*, right-click on the object CANDYBAR_DIM and click on the Column Properties... menu item, shown below:

When the editor appears, click the column on which you want to make a comment, click on the Comment tab and fill in your column comment in the input box provided, shown below. You can continue this process by clicking on each column in turn filling in the input box. Click Close to save your comment(s) and dismiss the editor.

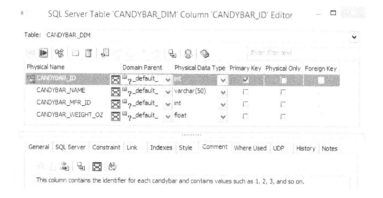

Next, let's generate the DDL to create the table as well as the comments as extended properties. First, click on Actions...Forward Engineer...Schema, shown below.

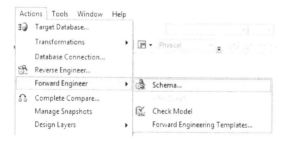

When the Forward Engineer Schema Generation dialog box appears, shown below, click on Other Options in the pane on the left and ensure that both Comments and Schema are checked. If not, check them before moving on.

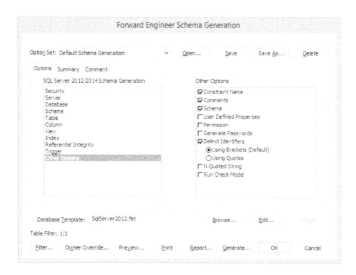

Now, click on the Preview... button at the bottom of the dialog box and the SQL Server DDL will be displayed, shown below.

```
CREATE TABLE [dbo].[CANDYBAR_DIM]
(
        [CANDYBAR_ID]        int  NOT NULL ,
        [CANDYBAR_NAME]      varchar(50)  NULL ,
        [CANDYBAR_MFR_ID]    int  NULL ,
        [CANDYBAR_WEIGHT_OZ] float  NULL
)
go

ALTER TABLE [dbo].[CANDYBAR_DIM]
        ADD CONSTRAINT [XPKCANDYBAR_DIM] PRIMARY KEY
CLUSTERED ([CANDYBAR_ID] ASC)
go

EXEC sp_addextendedproperty
@name = 'MS_Description', @value = 'This table contains a list
of candybars used in the Candybar Study. ',
@level0type = 'SCHEMA', @level0name = 'dbo',
@level1type = 'TABLE', @level1name = 'CANDYBAR_DIM'
go

EXEC sp_addextendedproperty
@name = 'MS_Description', @value = 'This column contains the
```

As you can see, several sp_addextendedproperty stored procedures are being called, the first for the table CANDYBAR_DIM and the second for the column CANDYBAR_ID. Take note that ERwin uses the extended property name MS_Description rather than Description used in the previous section. If you're planning on reverse engineering using ERwin, or other database design tool, you may want to stick with their name. This isn't a problem for us since the SQL shown in Chapter 2, *The Data Dictionary and Microsoft Word* can be altered to include any extended property name.

Next, let's do the same thing for Oracle. The only difference, besides choosing the appropriate target database, is that schema is not an option in the Other Options dialog box, but Comments still needs to be checked.

By clicking on the Preview... button, the Oracle Schema Generation Preview dialog appears displaying the DDL used to create the table as well as the comments, shown below.

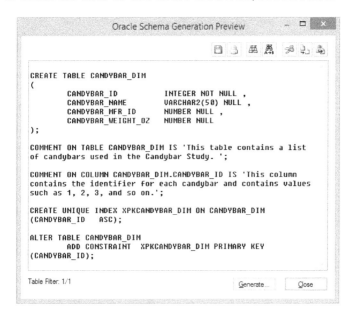

Home-Grown Data Dictionary Software

While you can code your own program to generate a nicely formatted data dictionary by yourself, a quick Google search brings up several home-grown suggestions. One suggestion is from Mr. SQL's blog entitled "Automatically Generate a Data Dictionary Using Extended Properties" and is SQL Server-specific. You can find the code on his blog here: mrsql.wordpress.com/2011/02/23/automatically-generating-a-data-dictionary-using-extended-properties/. I won't go through Mr. SQL's code, but I will show you the output generated by it:

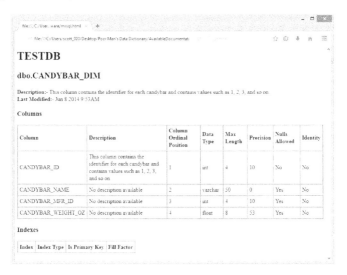

As you can see, the extended property associated with the table is shown next to the word Description and the extended property associated with the column CANDYBAR_ID is shown under the column Description in the table above. Note that the caveats I created are not shown. Mr. SQL's code also shows indexes, but since I haven't defined any indexes, the output is blank. Note that Mr. SQL's code also shows stored procedures (but not functions), as shown below, but since I have not placed any extended properties on these stored procedures, the text *No description available* is shown instead.

Stored Procedures

Stored Procedure	Description	Last Modified Date
INSERT_COUNTRY	No description available	Jan 7 2015 11:03AM
DOSTUFF	No description available	Jan 7 2015 11:06AM

Unfortunately, this code only produces a data dictionary in HTML format, does not allow for any modification of extended properties themselves, and only works for SQL Server.

Data Dictionary Creator

Data Dictionary Creator, available for free at datadictionary. codeplex.com, is a SQL Server-specific application which allows you to enter in table and column descriptions that are subsequently stored as extended properties in SQL Server. An example of its interface is shown below:

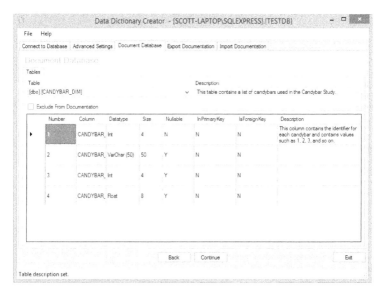

While this is a very nice application, it does have several drawbacks as compared to the method outlined in this book:

1. It does not interact with any other database besides SQL Server.
2. While you can capture one or more caveats at the column-level (by adding additional columns to the right of the Descriptions column shown above), you cannot enter in caveats at the table-level.
3. Stored procedures and functions are not included in this application's interface and are not displayed in the generated documentation.
4. Both table- and column-level descriptions are stored with the extended property name MS_Description.
5. This application fills in the extended properties as you complete a table or column description rather than a button which allows you to update the database when you see fit.

Data Dictionary Creator can generate documentation by clicking on the Export Now button on the Export Documentation tab. Although the application can generate Excel, Word, HTML, XML and T-SQL, here is an example of the generated HTML:

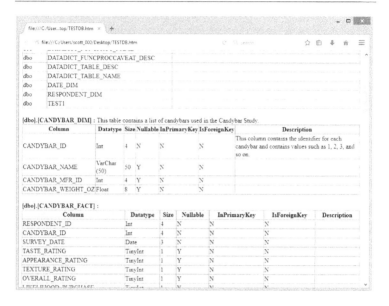

SQL Data Dictionary

Similar to Data Dictionary Creator outlined above, SQL Data Dictionary, available at www.sqldatadictionary.com for $US200/license, is a SQL Server-specific application which allows you to enter in table and column descriptions that are subsequently stored as extended properties in SQL Server.

Here is an example of its interface:

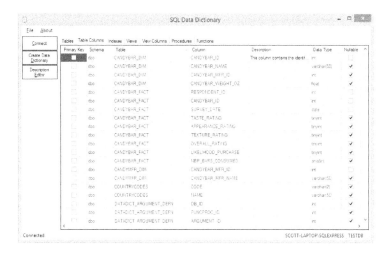

While this application is quite nice, it suffers from some of the same drawbacks as Data Dictionary Creator:

1. It does not interact with any other database besides SQL Server.
2. You cannot capture caveats.
3. Stored procedures and functions are included in this application's interface and you can enter in descriptions for both. While descriptions for stored procedures are successfully stored in the database as extended properties, descriptions for functions fail to be stored.
4. Both stored procedures and functions are not included in the generated data dictionary output, but mention of them is made under any dependent table.
5. Both table- and column-level descriptions are stored with the extended property name MS_Description.
6. This application fills in the extended properties as you complete a table or column description rather than a button which allows you to update the database when you see fit.

SQL Data Dictionary generates output in PDF, HTML and XML. For example, here is the output for CANDYBAR_DIM:

Table dbo.**CANDYBAR_DIM** *(0 rows)*

This table contains a list of candybars used in the Candybar Study.

Column	Data Type	Identity	Nullable	Default
CANDYBAR_ID	int			
This column contains the identifier for each candybar and contains values such as 1, 2, 3, and so on.				
CANDYBAR_NAME	varchar(50)		X	
CANDYBAR_MFR_ID	int		X	
CANDYBAR_WEIGHT_OZ	float		X	

And, here's the output for the table COUNTRYCODES. Take note that both stored procedures DOSTUFF and INSERT_COUNTRY make use of this table and are displayed in the output below:

Table dbo.**COUNTRYCODES** *(3 rows)*

Column	Data Type	Identity	Nullable	Default
CODE	varchar(2)		X	
NAME	varchar(50)		X	

Used by:

Procedure dbo.DOSTUFF

Procedure dbo.INSERT_COUNTRY

ApexSQL Doc

ApexSQL Doc, available at www.apexsql.com, is a SQL Server-specific application which allows you to enter in table, column, function, stored procedure, parameter, etc. descriptions that are subsequently stored as extended properties in SQL Server. ApexSQL Doc comes in three flavors:

1. Community Edition – this is free, but is limited. See the ApexSQL website for more.
2. Developer Edition – this costs US$249/user.
3. Professional Edition – this costs US$399/user and contains all of the features available.

The image below shows me editing the column CANDYBAR_MFR_ID from the CANDYBAR_DIM table:

Note that, unlike the previous software discussed, there's an Apply button, clearly shown in the image above, which allows you to save the descriptions to SQL Server when you are ready.

Note that you can choose to edit an existing extended property name, indicated by the drop-down box at the top of the image above, or you can create your own extended property names.

ApexSQL Doc allows you to generate a data dictionary in the following formats: Compiled Help File (.chm), Linked HTML (.html), Word 97-2003 (.doc), Word 2007 (.docx), and Portable Document Format (.pdf). Below is an example of a portion of the output from the Compiled Help File for the table CANDYBAR_DIM:

⬚ Table: TESTDB.dbo.CANDYBAR_DIM

− Collapse all

+ Description

+ Table properties

+ Creation options

− Columns

Name	Description	Data type	Max length	Nullable
CANDYBAR_ID	This column contains the identifier for each candybar and contains values such as 1, 2, 3, and so on.	int	4	
CANDYBAR_NAME		varchar	50	✓
CANDYBAR_MFR_ID	Now is the time...	int	4	✓
CANDYBAR_WEIGHT_OZ		float	8	✓

Total: 4 column(s)

− Extended properties

Name	Value
Caveat_1	This is a dangerous table!
Caveat_2	This is a very dangerous table!
Caveat_3	DANGER!!
Description	This table contains a list of candybars used in the Candybar Study.
MS_Description	This table contains a list of candybars used in the Candybar Study.

The output is customizable, even allowing you to provide a CSS stylesheet of your own! The output also shows the CREATE TABLE syntax for each table as well as the T-SQL code for each stored procedure and function.

While this application has many more features as compared to the software shown above, it suffers from a few minor drawbacks:

1. It does not interact with any other database besides SQL Server.
2. You cannot capture caveats except as additional extended properties (see the Extended Properties section in the image above).

Redgate SQL Doc

Redgate SQL Doc, available at www.red-gate.com, is a SQL Server-specific application which allows you to enter in table, column, function, stored procedure, parameter, etc. descriptions that are subsequently stored as extended properties in SQL Server. Redgate SQL Doc costs

US$369/user and is included in their SQL Developer Bundle for US$1,895/user.

A very nice feature of Redgate SQL Doc, not appearing in the other software mentioned in this chapter, is the integration with SQL Server Management Studio. In the image below, the menu item Document appears when you right-click on a table, stored procedure or function. This will bring up the Redgate SQL Doc software.

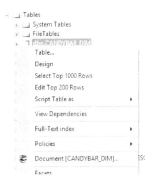

Shown below is the Redgate SQL Doc interface with the column CANDYBAR_MFR_ID being edited:

Similar to ApexSQL Doc, you can save the extended property to the database by clicking on the database icon, or cancel the change by clicking on the red X button. If you have made a change to the description and subsequently moved to a new field, these two images continued to be displayed as a reminder.

Redgate SQL Doc generates output in HTML, Word (.doc, .docx), Compiled Help (.chm) and PDF (.pdf) formats. Here is an example of the HTML output for the table CANDYBAR_DIM:

While this application is very nice, it does suffer from some drawbacks:

1. It does not interact with any other database besides SQL Server.
2. You cannot capture caveats.
3. Both table- and column-level descriptions are stored with the extended property name MS_Description.

Adivo Techwriter

Adivo Techwriter, available at www.adivo.com, is an application which allows you to enter in table, column, function, stored procedure, parameters, etc. descriptions as well as table-level remarks. Adivo Techwriter costs US$179/user and interacts with Microsoft Access, SQL Server, DB2, MySQL, Oracle, PostgreSQL and SAS.

Below is the Add New Source dialog box indicating the databases Adivo Techwriter interacts with:

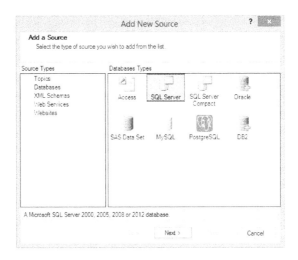

And here's a portion of the interface with the column CANDYBAR_MFR_ID being edited:

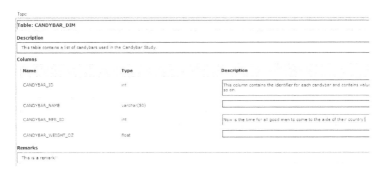

Techwriter generates documentation in the following formats: PDF Document (.pdf), Compiled Help File (.chm), HTML webpage (.html), Framed HTML webpage (.htm), Microsoft Word (.doc), XML DocBook (.xml), XML Paper Specification (.xps). Below is an example of the HTML output:

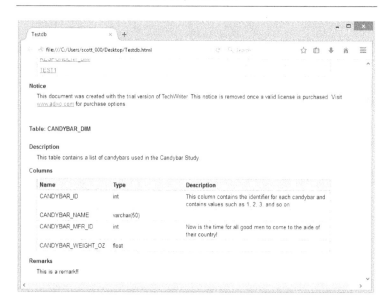

While this application is very nice, it does suffer from some drawbacks:

1. It does not save the table, column, etc. descriptions directly to the database. Rather, you generate a file containing the appropriate SQL code for your database.   For SQL Server, that's extended properties; for Oracle, it's COMMENTs; and so on. You then run this code in the database yourself.

2. You cannot capture caveats. Despite the ability to create a *remark* on a table, that remark is stored within the description of the table itself.

3. For SQL Server, all descriptions are stored with an extended property name of MS_Description.

Appendix

Oracle/SQL Server Metadata SQL Code

```
--SQL Server
SELECT A.TABLE_NAME,A.COLUMN_NAME,
    CASE
      WHEN A.DATA_TYPE='int' THEN 'INT'
      WHEN A.DATA_TYPE='bigint' THEN 'BIGINT'
      WHEN A.DATA_TYPE='smallint' THEN 'SMALLINT'
      WHEN A.DATA_TYPE='tinyint' THEN 'TINYINT'
      WHEN A.DATA_TYPE='float' THEN 'FLOAT'
      WHEN A.DATA_TYPE='real' THEN 'REAL'
      WHEN A.DATA_TYPE='date' THEN 'DATE'
      WHEN A.DATA_TYPE='smalldatetime' THEN 'SMALLDATETIME'
      WHEN A.DATA_TYPE='datetime' THEN 'DATETIME'
      WHEN A.DATA_TYPE='datetime2' THEN 'DATETIME2'
      WHEN A.DATA_TYPE='time' THEN 'TIME'
      WHEN A.DATA_TYPE='varchar'
          THEN 'VARCHAR('
              + CONVERT(VARCHAR,CHARACTER_MAXIMUM_LENGTH) + ')'
    END AS DATTYP,
    CASE WHEN A.IS_NULLABLE='YES' THEN 'NULL'
        WHEN A.IS_NULLABLE='NO' THEN 'NOT NULL'
    END AS NULLRES,
    DENSE_RANK() OVER (ORDER BY A.TABLE_NAME) as TABLE_NUM,
    COUNT(*) OVER (PARTITION BY A.TABLE_NAME) as TOTAL_COLS,
    B.TOTAL_TABLES
    FROM TESTDB.INFORMATION_SCHEMA.COLUMNS A,
        (SELECT COUNT(DISTINCT TABLE_NAME) AS TOTAL_TABLES
          FROM TESTDB.INFORMATION_SCHEMA.Columns
          WHERE TABLE_NAME IN (...subset for tables here...)) B
    WHERE A.TABLE_NAME IN (...subset for tables here...)
    ORDER BY A.TABLE_NAME,A.ORDINAL_POSITION;

--Oracle
SELECT TABLE_NAME,
      COLUMN_NAME,
      CASE
        WHEN DATA_TYPE='DATE' THEN 'DATE'
        WHEN DATA_TYPE='VARCHAR2'
            THEN 'VARCHAR2(' || TO_CHAR(DATA_LENGTH) || ')'
          WHEN DATA_TYPE='NUMBER' AND DATA_PRECISION IS NOT NULL
            THEN 'NUMBER(' || TO_CHAR(DATA_PRECISION)
                          || ',' || TO_CHAR(DATA_SCALE) || ')'
          WHEN DATA_TYPE='NUMBER' AND DATA_PRECISION IS NULL
            THEN 'NUMBER'
        WHEN DATA_TYPE='BLOB' THEN 'BLOB'
        WHEN DATA_TYPE='ROWID' THEN 'ROWID'
        WHEN DATA_TYPE='CHAR'
            THEN 'CHAR(' || TO_CHAR(DATA_LENGTH) || ')'
        ELSE 'UNKNOWN'
        END AS DATTYP,
        CASE
        WHEN NULLABLE='N' THEN 'NOT NULL'
        WHEN NULLABLE='Y' THEN 'NULL'
        ELSE 'NULL?'
        END AS NULLRES,
        DENSE_RANK() OVER (ORDER BY TABLE_NAME) as TABLE_NUM,
        COUNT(*) OVER (PARTITION BY TABLE_NAME) as TOTAL_COLS,
        COUNT(DISTINCT TABLE_NAME) OVER () as TOTAL_TABLES
  FROM ALL_TAB_COLUMNS
```

```
WHERE (OWNER='enter-schema-name-here'
ORDER BY TABLE_NAME,COLUMN_ID;
```

Oracle/SQL Server Data Dictionary Tables

```
--SQL Server
CREATE TABLE DATADICT_DB_DEFN(DB_ID int,
                              DB_NAME varchar(30))

CREATE TABLE DATADICT_TABLE_NAME(DB_ID int,
                                 TABLE_ID int,
                                 TABLE_NAME varchar(30))

CREATE TABLE DATADICT_TABLE_DESC(DB_ID int,
                                 TABLE_ID int,
                                 TABLE_DESC varchar(2000))

CREATE TABLE DATADICT_COLUMN_DEFN(DB_ID int,
                                  TABLE_ID int,
                                  COLUMN_ID int,
                                  COLUMN_NAME varchar(30),
                                  DATA_TYPE varchar(20),
                                  NULLABILITY varchar(10))

CREATE TABLE DATADICT_COLUMN_DESC(DB_ID int,
                                  TABLE_ID int,
                                  COLUMN_ID int,
                                  COLUMN_NAME varchar(30),
                                  COLUMN_DESC varchar(2000))

CREATE TABLE DATADICT_CAVEAT_DESC(DB_ID int,
                                  TABLE_ID int,
                                  CAVEAT_ID int,
                                  CAVEAT_DESC varchar(2000))

CREATE TABLE DATADICT_FUNCPROC_NAME(DB_ID int,
                                    FUNCPROC_ID int,
                                    FUNCPROC_TYPE varchar(1),
                                    FUNCPROC_NAME varchar(30))

CREATE TABLE DATADICT_FUNCPROC_DESC(DB_ID int,
                                    FUNCPROC_ID int,
                                    FUNCPROC_DESC varchar(2000))

CREATE TABLE DATADICT_FUNCPROCCAVEAT_DESC(DB_ID int,
                                          FUNCPROC_ID int,
                                          CAVEAT_ID int,
                                          CAVEAT_DESC varchar(2000))

CREATE TABLE DATADICT_ARGUMENT_DESC(DB_ID int,
                                    FUNCPROC_ID int,
                                    ARGUMENT_ID int,
                                    ARGUMENT_NAME varchar(30),
                                    ARGUMENT_DESC varchar(2000))

CREATE TABLE DATADICT_ARGUMENT_DEFN(DB_ID int,
                                    FUNCPROC_ID int,
                                    ARGUMENT_ID int,
                                    ARGUMENT_NAME varchar(30),
                                    DIRECTION varchar(6),
                                    DATATYPE varchar(10))

CREATE TABLE DATADICT_CODEFRAGMENTS_DESC(DB_ID int,
                                         TABLE_ID int,
                                         FRAGMENT_ID int,
```

```
                                 FRAGMENT_LINE int,
                                 FRAGMENT_DESC varchar(2000),
                                 FRAGMENT_CODE varchar(2000))


--Oracle
CREATE TABLE DATADICT_DB_DEFN(DB_ID NUMBER,
                             DB_NAME VARCHAR2(30));

CREATE TABLE DATADICT_CAVEAT_DESC(DB_ID NUMBER,
                                 TABLE_ID NUMBER,
                                 CAVEAT_ID NUMBER,
                                 CAVEAT_DESC VARCHAR2(2000))


CREATE TABLE DATADICT_COLUMN_DEFN(DB_ID NUMBER,
                                 TABLE_ID NUMBER,
                                 COLUMN_ID NUMBER,
                                 COLUMN_NAME VARCHAR2(30),
                                 DATA_TYPE VARCHAR2(20),
                                 NULLABILITY VARCHAR2(10))


CREATE TABLE DATADICT_COLUMN_DESC(DB_ID NUMBER,
                                 TABLE_ID NUMBER,
                                 COLUMN_ID NUMBER,
                                 COLUMN_NAME VARCHAR2(30),
                                 COLUMN_DESC VARCHAR2(2000))


CREATE TABLE DATADICT_TABLE_DESC(DB_ID NUMBER,
                                TABLE_ID NUMBER,
                                TABLE_DESC VARCHAR2(2000))

CREATE TABLE DATADICT_TABLE_NAME(DB_ID NUMBER,
                                TABLE_ID NUMBER,
                                TABLE_NAME VARCHAR2(30))

CREATE TABLE DATADICT_FUNCPROC_NAME(DB_ID NUMBER,
                                   FUNCPROC_ID NUMBER,
                                   FUNCPROC_TYPE VARCHAR2(1),
                                   FUNCPROC_NAME VARCHAR2(30))

CREATE TABLE DATADICT_FUNCPROC_DESC(DB_ID NUMBER,
                                   FUNCPROC_ID NUMBER,
                                   FUNCPROC_DESC VARCHAR2(2000))

CREATE TABLE DATADICT_FUNCPROCCAVEAT_DESC(DB_ID NUMBER,
                                         FUNCPROC_ID NUMBER,
                                         CAVEAT_ID NUMBER,
                                         CAVEAT_DESC VARCHAR2(2000))

CREATE TABLE DATADICT_ARGUMENT_DESC(DB_ID NUMBER,
                                   FUNCPROC_ID NUMBER,
                                   ARGUMENT_ID NUMBER,
                                   ARGUMENT_NAME VARCHAR2(30),
                                   ARGUMENT_DESC VARCHAR2(2000))

CREATE TABLE DATADICT_ARGUMENT_DEFN(DB_ID NUMBER,
                                   FUNCPROC_ID NUMBER,
                                   ARGUMENT_ID NUMBER,
                                   ARGUMENT_NAME VARCHAR2(30),
                                   DIRECTION VARCHAR2(6),
                                   DATATYPE VARCHAR2(10))

CREATE TABLE DATADICT_CODEFRAGMENTS_DESC(DB_ID NUMBER,
                                        TABLE_ID NUMBER,
                                        FRAGMENT_ID NUMBER,
```

```
                          FRAGMENT_LINE NUMBER,
                          FRAGMENT_DESC VARCHAR2(2000),
                          FRAGMENT_CODE VARCHAR2(2000))
```

Proactive Checker SQL Code

```
--Oracle Only
--Table mis-matches
SELECT CASE
       WHEN A.TABLE_NAME IS NOT NULL
            AND B.TABLE_NAME IS NULL THEN '*****NEW*****'
       WHEN A.TABLE_NAME IS NULL
            AND B.TABLE_NAME IS NOT NULL THEN '*****DEL*****'
       WHEN A.TABLE_NAME IS NOT NULL
            AND B.TABLE_NAME IS NOT NULL THEN '*****BOTH****'
       END AS ACTION,
       A.TABLE_NAME AS ORACLE_TABLE_NAME,
       B.TABLE_NAME AS DICT_TABLE_NAME
 FROM ALL_TABLES A FULL OUTER JOIN DATADICT_TABLE_NAME B
 ON A.TABLE_NAME=B.TABLE_NAME
WHERE A.OWNER IS NULL
       OR A.OWNER='enter-schema-name-here'
 ORDER BY 1,2;

--Column mis-matches
SELECT CASE
       WHEN A.COLUMN_NAME IS NOT NULL
            AND B.COLUMN_NAME IS NULL THEN '*****NEW*****'
       WHEN A.COLUMN_NAME IS NULL
            AND B.COLUMN_NAME IS NOT NULL THEN '*****DEL*****'
       WHEN A.COLUMN_NAME IS NOT NULL
            AND B.COLUMN_NAME IS NOT NULL THEN '*****BOTH****'
       END AS ACTION,
       A.TABLE_NAME AS ORACLE_TABLE_NAME,
       A.COLUMN_NAME AS ORACLE_COLUMN_NAME,
       B.TABLE_NAME AS DICT_TABLE_NAME,
       B.COLUMN_NAME AS DICT_COLUMN_NAME
 FROM ALL_TAB_COLUMNS A FULL OUTER JOIN (
   SELECT Y.TABLE_NAME,X.COLUMN_NAME
    FROM DATADICT_COLUMN_DEFN X INNER JOIN DATADICT_TABLE_NAME Y
   ON X.DB_ID=Y.DB_ID
       AND X.TABLE_ID=Y.TABLE_ID) B
 ON A.TABLE_NAME=B.TABLE_NAME
    AND A.COLUMN_NAME=B.COLUMN_NAME
WHERE A.OWNER IS NULL
       OR A.OWNER='enter-schema-name-here'
 ORDER BY 1,2;

--Data Type and Nullability mis-matches
SELECT CASE
       WHEN A.DATTYP=B.DATA_TYPE THEN '*****MATCH*****'
       ELSE '*****MIS-MATCH*****'
       END AS DATA_TYPE_ACTION,
       CASE
       WHEN A.NULLRES=B.NULLABILITY THEN '*****MATCH*****'
       ELSE '*****MIS-MATCH*****'
       END AS NULLABILITY_ACTION,
       A.TABLE_NAME AS ORACLE_TABLE_NAME,
       A.COLUMN_NAME AS ORACLE_COLUMN_NAME,
       A.DATTYP AS ORACLE_DATA_TYPE,
       A.NULLRES AS ORACLE_NULLABILITY,
       B.TABLE_NAME AS DICT_TABLE_NAME,
       B.COLUMN_NAME AS DICT_COLUMN_NAME,
       B.DATA_TYPE AS DICT_DATA_TYPE,
```

```
      B.NULLABILITY AS DICT_NULLABILITY
FROM (
      SELECT TABLE_NAME,COLUMN_NAME,
      CASE
        WHEN DATA_TYPE='DATE' THEN 'DATE'
        WHEN DATA_TYPE='VARCHAR2'
             THEN 'VARCHAR2(' || TO_CHAR(DATA_LENGTH) || ')'
        WHEN DATA_TYPE='NUMBER' AND DATA_PRECISION IS NOT NULL
             THEN 'NUMBER(' || TO_CHAR(DATA_PRECISION)
                           || ',' || TO_CHAR(DATA_SCALE) || ')'
        WHEN DATA_TYPE='NUMBER' AND DATA_PRECISION IS NULL
             THEN 'NUMBER'
        WHEN DATA_TYPE='BLOB' THEN 'BLOB'
        WHEN DATA_TYPE='ROWID' THEN 'ROWID'
        WHEN DATA_TYPE='CHAR'
             THEN 'CHAR(' || TO_CHAR(DATA_LENGTH) || ')'
        ELSE 'UNKNOWN'
        END AS DATTYP,
      CASE
        WHEN NULLABLE='N' THEN 'NOT NULL'
        WHEN NULLABLE='Y' THEN 'NULL'
        ELSE 'NULL?'
        END AS NULLRES
        FROM ALL_TAB_COLUMNS
        WHERE OWNER='enter-schema-name-here'
      ) A
    FULL OUTER JOIN
    (
     SELECT Y.TABLE_NAME,X.COLUMN_NAME,
            X.DATA_TYPE,X.NULLABILITY
      FROM DATADICT_COLUMN_DEFN X
           INNER JOIN DATADICT_TABLE_NAME Y
       ON X.DB_ID=Y.DB_ID
          AND X.TABLE_ID=Y.TABLE_ID
     ) B
ON A.TABLE_NAME=B.TABLE_NAME
   AND A.COLUMN_NAME=B.COLUMN_NAME
ORDER BY 1,2;
```

Index